# *Wie sagt man...?*

## A NEW VOCABULARY FOR GCSE GERMAN

*Robert Mathews*

Hodder & Stoughton

A MEMBER OF THE HODDER HEADLINE GROUP

*British Library Cataloguing in Publication Data*

A catalogue record for this title is available from the British Library

ISBN 0 340 65553 4

First published 1997
Impression number     10 9 8 7 6 5 4 3 2 1
Year           2001 2000 1999 1998 1997

Printed in Great Britain for Hodder & Stoughton Educational, a division of
Hodder Headline Plc, 338 Euston Road, London NW1 3BH by Cox & Wyman
Ltd, Reading, Berkshire.

# Wie sagt man...?

A NEW VOCABULARY FOR GCSE GERMAN

Robert Mathews

# Contents

# CONTENTS

# Introduction

*Wie sagt man...?* aims to help you to prepare for your German examinations by providing a comprehensive listing of words and phrases. You can use the book as part of your course of study (particularly when preparing for written or oral work), and as a revision aid when the exams approach.

## The organisation of the book

The book is divided into five main themes: Everyday activities, Personal and social life, The world around us, The world of work and The international world. Students preparing for GCSE will perhaps already be familiar with these main themes as they relate to the National Curriculum Areas of Experience. Those of you preparing for other exams will simply find that these themes provide a logical framework for learning vocabulary.

Each of these themes is divided into a number of sub-sections. A full list of these is given in the contents list. When you want to find several words on the same topic, you can easily find the right section in the list of contents, and most of the words you are likely to need will be there.

The vocabulary itself is presented in a sequence that follows logical thought processes. Where some useful related vocabulary appears in a separate section, cross-references (⟶) have been given to direct you to this.

The definite article (*der*, *die* or *das*) has been used unless it is more natural to use a word with the indefinite article (*ein*, *eine*, or *ein*). Wherever gender may be unclear, an indication, (*m*), (*f*) or (*n*) is given, and if the noun is plural it is indicated (*pl*). Plurals forms are given in brackets after the noun. Do not ignore the genders and plurals. At first they may seem random, but the more you learn, the more they will fit into a pattern and the fewer mistakes you will make. Your teacher will be able to help you spot some patterns.

The conjugation of strong verbs (excluding *sein*, *gehen* and *werden*) has been given in the third person singular form except in phrases.

The following abbreviations have also been used throughout the book:

| | |
|---|---|
| *adj.* | adjective |
| *adj. noun* | adjectival noun: a noun which works like an adjective, eg *der Deutsche, ein Deutscher.* |
| *m* | masculine/male |
| *f* | feminine/female |
| *n* | neuter |
| *sg* | singular |
| *pl* | plural |
| * | perfect tense formed with *sein* |
| *Acc* | takes Accusative case |
| *Dat* | takes Dative case |
| *+clause* | takes clause |
| *+verb* | takes verb |
| *intransitive* | intransitive verb (a verb which does not have an object in the Accusative, eg *ich schlafe hier; er hilft mir*). |
| *transitive* | transitive verb (a verb which has an object in the Accusative, eg *wir kennen sie; ich finde es*). |
| *irreg* | irregular verb |
| *insep* | inseparable verb |
| *sep* | separable verb |
| *s* | strong verb |
| *w* | weak verb |

Masculine nouns with (-n, -n) after them end in -n in all cases (in the singular and plural) except for the nominative singular. These are called weak masculine nouns.

## *Jetzt bist du dran!* vocabulary practice

These regular vocabulary practice activities will help you to test yourself, and will encourage you to scan the preceding lists looking for words that do not come to you straight away. The process of looking over these words will help you to remember them, just as an advertiser gets you to remember a message by showing it to you rapidly over and over again. The answers to the practice activities are given at the back of the book for you to check. You could also devise your own activities to test yourself – or a friend.

## GCSE candidates

The GCSE examination boards specify a minimum core vocabulary required to achieve a Foundation-level pass, and *Wie sagt man...?* provides the core vocabulary requirements of all the GCSE boards. As these core requirements vary from board to board, vocabulary has not been artificially separated or highlighted. Remember that your best strategy for success is to absorb as much vocabulary as you can...

## Learning vocabulary

You will not need to know all the words in the book, but if you aim to learn as many as possible, you will be well on the way to giving yourself the best opportunity to reach the highest possible level in your German exam. Although in some examinations you may be allowed to refer to a dictionary, when you are listening or speaking, you cannot constantly look up words – not only can you waste valuable time, you may also – in the heat of the moment – choose the wrong word! To avoid this happening, here are some tips for effective vocabulary learning...

* Go somewhere you can find peace and quiet. Other noises, especially talking, can be very distracting.

* Little and often. Don't try to learn huge amounts in long, intense sessions or your brain will become overloaded! Every time you return to a section of vocabulary it will become more and more familiar. Six five-minute sessions are far more valuable than a half-hour stretch.

* It often helps to make up a sentence so that a word has a context – you have actually made the word work for you by making it convey information. Just a short sentence will do.

* *Saying* a word or phrase aloud (even in a whisper) means that you are hearing it as well as seeing it, and so it has two routes into your brain.

* Writing vocabulary out helps many people – that's a third route into the brain.

* Always learn the gender (and irregular plural) with the noun, and practise these by including them in sentences.

* Learn the words German to English first. Cover up the English words to test yourself, then try the other way round.

* Look for resemblances to other words in English, French or any other languages you are learning. Even if the similarities are pure coincidences, they can still help.

* Try learning with a friend who is working towards the same exam. Test each other, taking it in turns from German to English, and then from English into German.

* Revise regularly what you have already learned, otherwise your hard work will easily be lost.

* Don't be put off if you have forgotten much of what you thought you had learned. Photographic memories are very rare indeed!

And finally, remember that it is very difficult to communicate effectively in German or indeed to do well in a German exam if you do not have the words ready. Imagine having to look up the fingering for every other note when playing a piece of music. As in music, the hard work you put into learning things will give you far more control and a greater sense of achievement. Remember too that you need both language skills and the raw material called vocabulary to achieve success. Your teacher and your course books are there to provide language skills, this book contains the raw materials, carefully sorted and labelled. It will serve you best if you open it often!

*Alles Gute!*

*Robert Mathews*

# A: Everyday activities

## 1 Zeitausdrücke     Time expressions

### a Die Tage     Days of the week

|  |  |
|---|---|
| der Tag (-e) | day |
| der Sonntag | Sunday |
| der Montag | Monday |
| der Dienstag | Tuesday |
| der Mittwoch | Wednesday |
| der Donnerstag | Thursday |
| der Freitag | Friday |
| der Samstag<br>der Sonnabend } | Saturday |

|  |  |
|---|---|
| sonntags usw | regularly on Sundays etc |
| wir gehen samstags abends in die Stadt | we go into town on Saturday evenings |

|  |  |
|---|---|
| der Wochentag | weekday |
| der Werktag | working day |
| der Feiertag | public, bank holiday |
| feiertags (an Feiertagen) | on Bank Holidays |
| die Woche (-n) | week |
| pro Woche<br>in der Woche } | per week |
| zwei Wochen | fortnight |
| das Wochenende (-n) | weekend |
| am Wochenende | at the weekend |

|  |  |
|---|---|
| letzten Montag<br>vorigen Montag } | last Monday |
| vor (drei Tagen) | (three days) ago |
| letzten Monat | last month |
| letzte Woche | last week |
| nächste Woche | next week |
| morgen in acht Tagen | a week tomorrow |
| nächsten Monat | next month |
| nächstes Jahr | next year |
| nächsten Sonntag | next Sunday |
| ab nächstem Sonntag | from next Sunday onwards |
| bis Sonntag | until/by Sunday |

| | |
|---|---|
| jeden Sonntag | each Sunday |
| eines Tages | one day |

### b Die Monate — Months

| | |
|---|---|
| der Monat (-e) | month |
| der Januar | January |
| der Februar | February |
| der März | March |
| der April | April |
| der Mai | May |
| der Juni | June |
| der Juli | July |
| der August | August |
| der September | September |
| der Oktober | October |
| der November | November |
| der Dezember | December |

| | |
|---|---|
| im Januar | in January |
| vorigen Dezember / letzten Dezember | last December |
| nächsten Juli | next July |
| jeden September | every September |

| | |
|---|---|
| das Datum | date |
| der wievielte ist es? / den wievielten haben wir? | what is the date? |
| es ist der erste Januar / wir haben den ersten Januar | it's the first of January |

### c Die Jahreszeiten — Seasons

| | |
|---|---|
| die Jahreszeit (-en) | season |
| der Frühling / das Frühjahr | spring |
| der Sommer | summer |
| der Herbst | autumn |
| der Winter | winter |
| im Winter usw | in winter etc |

### d Die Jahre — Years

| | |
|---|---|
| das Jahr (-e) | year |
| letztes Jahr | last year |

| | |
|---|---|
| dieses Jahr | this year |
| nächstes Jahr | next year |
| ich bin 1982 geboren<br>ich bin im Jahre 1982 geboren } | I was born in 1982 |
| im Jahre 2000<br>2000 } | in 2000 |
| das Jahrzehnt (-e) | decade |
| das Jahrhundert (-e) | century |
| im zwanzigsten Jahrhundert | in the twentieth century |

## e Die Tageszeiten    Times of day

| | |
|---|---|
| der Morgen | (*early*) morning |
| der Vormittag (-e) | morning |
| morgens<br>vormittags } | *regularly* in the morning |
| der Mittag | midday, noon |
| mittags | *regularly* at midday |
| der Nachmittag (-e) | afternoon |
| nachmittags | *regularly* in the afternoon |
| der Abend (-e) | evening |
| abends | *regularly* in the evening |
| die Nacht (¨e) | night |
| nachts | *regularly* at night |
| die Mitternacht | midnight |
| vorgestern | on the day before yesterday |
| gestern | yesterday |
| gestern abend | yesterday evening |
| diese Nacht<br>heute nacht } | last night (*with past tense*) |
| heute | today |
| heute morgen | this morning |
| heute abend | this evening |
| heute nacht<br>diese Nacht } | tonight (*with present or future tense*) |
| morgen | tomorrow |
| morgen früh | tomorrow morning |
| morgen nachmittag | tomorrow afternoon |
| am folgenden Tag | on the following day |
| übermorgen | on the day after tomorrow |

| | |
|---|---|
| früh | early |
| spät | late |
| früh morgens | early in the morning |

| | |
|---|---|
| spät am Abend | late in the evening |
| früher oder später | sooner or later |

| | |
|---|---|
| die Zeit | time (*in general*) |
| Zeit verbringen (*irreg w*) | to spend time |
| Zeit verschwenden | to waste time |
| vergehen (-s) | to pass by (*of time*) |

## Jetzt bist du dran! 1

*Welcher Tag ist es?* *What day is it?*

*Beispiel: Gestern war Donnerstag = Heute ist Freitag.*

1 *Morgen ist Donnerstag.*
2 *Gestern war Sonntag.*
3 *Übermorgen ist Montag.*
4 *Vorgestern war Mittwoch.*

5 *Vor drei Tagen war Samstag.*
6 *In drei Tagen ist Sonntag.*
7 *Übermorgen ist Dienstag.*

## f Die Uhrzeit — Time

| | |
|---|---|
| die Sekunde (-n) | second |
| die Minute (-n) | minute |
| jede Minute | at any minute |
| eine Viertelstunde | quarter of an hour |
| eine halbe Stunde | half an hour |
| eine Stunde (-n) | hour |
| eine Stunde lang | for an hour |

| | |
|---|---|
| der Augenblick (-e) } der Moment (-e) } | moment |
| im Augenblick | at the moment |
| eine Weile | for a while |
| eine ganze Weile | for a long time |
| dauern | to last |
| die Dauer | length, duration |
| wie lange dauert...? | how long does ... last? |
| wie lange braucht man, um ... zu machen? | how long does it take to...? |

| | |
|---|---|
| wie spät ist es? | what's the time? |
| es ist zwei Uhr | it's two o'clock |

| | |
|---|---|
| es ist halb drei | it's half past two |
| es ist Viertel nach vier | it's a quarter past four |
| es ist fünfundzwanzig Minuten nach fünf | it's twenty-five past five |
| es ist Viertel vor sieben | it's a quarter to seven |
| (die) Mitternacht | midnight |
| um Mitternacht | at midnight |

| | |
|---|---|
| um ein Uhr | at 1 o'clock |
| gegen Mittag/gegen ein Uhr | around midday/around 1 |
| es ist Punkt drei Uhr | it's exactly three o'clock |
| es ist erst drei Uhr | it's only three o'clock |
| um drei Uhr | at three o'clock |
| gegen drei Uhr | at about three o'clock |
| genau um drei Uhr | exactly at three o'clock |
| beinahe ⎫ fast ⎭ | almost |
| schon ⎫ bereits ⎭ | already |
| es ist schon drei Uhr vorbei | it's gone three already |
| meine Uhr geht (fünf Minuten) vor/nach | my watch is (five mins) fast/slow |
| schlagen (es schlägt) (s) | to strike |
| es schlägt drei | it is striking three |
| aufziehen (s; sep) | to wind up |

## Jetzt bist du dran! 2

*Wie spät ist es? Gib jedesmal zwei Antworten: eine Uhrzeit zwischen Mitternacht und Mittag, und eine andere zwischen Mittag und Mitternacht. Schreib die Antworten voll aus!*

*What time is it? Give two answers each time: one which shows a time between midnight and midday, another which shows a time between midday and midnight. Write your answers out in full.*

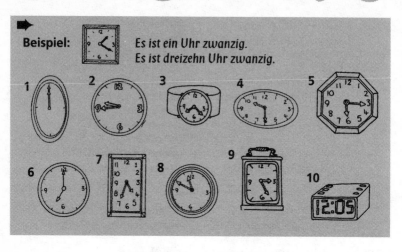

**Beispiel:** Es ist ein Uhr zwanzig.
Es ist dreizehn Uhr zwanzig.

## g Wie oft?    How often?

| | |
|---|---|
| **stündlich** | hourly, every hour |
| **täglich** | daily, every day |
| **alle zwei Tage** | every other day |
| **wöchentlich** | weekly, every week |
| **monatlich** | monthly, every month |
| **jährlich** | yearly, annual |
| **minutenlang** | for minutes on end |
| **stundenlang** | for hours on end |
| **tagelang** | for days on end |
| **wochenlang** | for weeks on end |
| **monatelang** | for months on end |
| **jahrelang** | for years on end |
| **das Mal (-e)** | occasion, time |
| **einmal** | once |
| **noch einmal** | once again |
| **zweimal** | twice |
| **einmal pro Woche** | once a week |
| **zweimal pro Monat** | twice a month |
| **immer** | always |
| **immer noch/noch immer** | still |
| **normalerweise** | normally |
| **meistens** | mostly |
| **gewöhnlich** | usually |
| **oft** | often |
| **häufig** | frequent(ly) |

| | |
|---|---|
| manchmal | sometimes |
| von Zeit zu Zeit | from time to time |
| selten | seldom, rarely, not often |
| nicht mehr | no longer |
| nie | never |

## h Wann? — When?

| | |
|---|---|
| damals | in those days, then |
| neulich | recently |
| jetzt } nun | now |
| heutzutage | nowadays |

| | |
|---|---|
| bevor (+*clause*) | before (*in time*) |
| bevor ich frühstücke | before I eat breakfast |
| vor (+*Dat*) | before, earlier than |
| vor dem Frühstück | before breakfast |
| während (+*Gen*) | during |
| gleich nach (+*Dat*) | just after (+*noun*) |
| kurz darauf } kurz danach | shortly afterwards |
| anschließend | next/after that |
| wenig später | not long afterwards |
| danach | after that |
| nach (+*Dat*) | after (+*noun*) |
| nachdem (+*clause*) | after (+ *clause*) |
| nachher | afterwards |
| etwas später | a little later |

| | |
|---|---|
| sofort | immediately |
| sogleich | straight away, immediately |
| bald | soon |
| sobald wie möglich | as soon as possible |
| gleich | in a moment |
| dann | then |
| irgendwann | some time or another |
| dann und wann } hin und wieder } ab und zu | now and again |

| | |
|---|---|
| zuerst | first of all, at first |
| am Anfang | at the beginning |
| schließlich | finally (*at end of list*) |

| | |
|---|---|
| endlich | at last |
| am Ende | at the end |

| | |
|---|---|
| auf einmal } plötzlich } | suddenly |
| schon } bereits } | already |
| noch nicht | not yet |
| erst (um Mitternacht) | not until, only (at midnight) |

| | |
|---|---|
| je | ever |
| in fünf Minuten | in five minutes |
| eine (ganze) Weile/Zeitlang | (quite) a while |
| lange | for a long time |
| vor einer Stunde | an hour ago |

| | |
|---|---|
| im allgemeinen | generally |
| nur | only |
| andauernd | continuously |

| | |
|---|---|
| seit | since |
| ich wohne seit zwei Jahren hier | I have been living here for two years |

| | |
|---|---|
| die Vergangenheit | past |
| in der Vergangenheit | in the past |
| die Gegenwart | present |
| zur Zeit | at present |
| die Zukunft | future |
| in (der) Zukunft | in (the) future |

## 2 Zahlen und Zeit  Numbers

### a Die Zahlen  Numbers

| | | | |
|---|---|---|---|
| null | 0 | neun | 9 |
| eins | 1 | zehn | 10 |
| zwei | 2 | elf | 11 |
| drei | 3 | zwölf | 12 |
| vier | 4 | dreizehn | 13 |
| fünf | 5 | vierzehn | 14 |
| sechs | 6 | fünfzehn | 15 |
| sieben | 7 | sechzehn | 16 |
| acht | 8 | siebzehn | 17 |

| | | | |
|---|---|---|---|
| achtzehn | 18 | hundert | 100 |
| neunzehn | 19 | hunderteins | 101 |
| zwanzig | 20 | hundertsiebenundzwanzig | 127 |
| einundzwanzig | 21 | zweihundert | 200 |
| zweiundzwanzig | 22 | zweihundertsechsundsiebzig | 276 |
| dreiundzwanzig | 23 | tausend | 1,000 |
| vierundzwanzig | 24 | tausendfünfhundertfünfzig | |
| fünfundzwanzig | 25 | (*as quantity*) | 1,550 |
| sechsundzwanzig | 26 | fünfzehnhundertfünfzig | |
| siebenundzwanzig | 27 | (*as date*) | 1550 |
| achtundzwanzig | 28 | neunzehnhundertsechsundneunzig | |
| neunundzwanzig | 29 | | 1996 |
| dreißig | 30 | zweitausendeins | 2,001 |
| vierzig | 40 | eine Million (-en) | |
| fünfzig | 50 | (1 Mio.) | 1,000,000 |
| sechzig | 60 | zwei Millionen | |
| siebzig | 70 | (2 Mio.) | 2,000,000 |
| achtzig | 80 | eine Milliarde (-n) | |
| neunzig | 90 | (1 Mrd.) | 1,000,000,000 |

## b Rechnen — Calculating

| | |
|---|---|
| addieren | to add |
| **3 plus 4 ist 7** | 3 plus 4 is 7 |
| subtrahieren | to subtract |
| **7 minus 4 ist 3** | 7 minus 4 is 3 |
| teilen/dividieren | to divide |
| **12 durch 4 ist 3** | 12 divided by 4 is 3 |
| multiplizieren | to multiply |
| **3 mal 4 ist 12** | 3 times 4 is 12 |

| | |
|---|---|
| ein Viertel (-) | ¼ |
| ein Drittel (-) | ⅓ |
| die Hälfte (-n) | ½ |
| zwei Drittel | ⅔ |
| drei Viertel | ¾ |
| eineinviertel | 1¼ |
| eineinhalb } anderthalb | 1½ |
| eindreiviertel | 1¾ |
| eins Komma sieben fünf (1,75) | 1.75 |

## Jetzt bist du dran! 3

| | |
|---|---|
| *Ein bißchen Rechnen!* | *A little arithmetic!* |
| *Schreib die Antworten voll aus!* | *Write the answers out in full.* |

*Beispiel: Elf plus vier mal zwei = dreißig*

1 sechs mal fünf
2 zweiundzwanzig mal vier
3 hundertdreißig durch zwei dividiert
4 zweitausend minus vierhundert durch acht
5 fünfhundert plus hundertfünfundzwanzig minus fünf mit drei multipliziert

6 achtzehn plus zweiundzwanzig plus einundsechzig
7 vierundsiebzig minus drei
8 viermal vierzig durch zwei dividiert
9 achtzig plus elf
10 zweihundert mal tausend

### c Ordinalzahlen    Ordinal numbers

These need articles to agree with the noun, eg *Sie nehmen **die** zweite Straße links. Er nimmt **ein** zweites Stück Kuchen.*

| | |
|---|---|
| **erste** | first |
| **zweite** | second |
| **dritte** | third |
| **vierte** | fourth |
| **fünfte** | fifth |
| **sechste** | sixth |
| **siebte** | seventh |
| **achte** | eighth |
| **neunte** | ninth |
| **zehnte** | tenth |
| **-te** (*up to 19th*) | -th |
| **zwanzigste** | twentieth |
| **einundzwanzigste** | twenty-first |
| **-ste** (*20th and above*) | -th |
| **hundertste** | hundredth |

## 3 Das tägliche Leben — Daily life

### a Vor der Schule — Before school

| | |
|---|---|
| aufwachen (*sep*) | to wake up (*intransitive*) |
| ich wache früh auf | I wake up early |
| wecken/aufwecken (*sep*) | to wake up (*transitive*) |
| das Radio weckt mich (auf) | the radio wakes me up |
| wach | awake |
| der Wecker (-) | alarm clock |
| der Radiowecker (-) | radio-alarm clock |
| läuten <br> klingeln } | to ring |
| aufstehen* (er steht ... auf) <br> (*s; sep*) | to get up |
| langsam | slowly |
| sofort | immediately |
| noch halb im Schlaf | still half asleep |
| müde | tired |
| gähnen | to yawn |

| | |
|---|---|
| das Badezimmer (-) <br> das Bad } | bathroom |
| ins Bad gehen* (*s*) | to go to the bathroom |
| die Badewanne | bath (tub) |
| ein Bad nehmen (er nimmt) (*s*) <br> (sich) baden } | to have a bath |
| (sich) duschen | to have a shower |
| sich waschen (er wäscht sich) (*s*) | to wash |
| schmutzig | dirty |
| dreckig | dirty, filthy |
| sauber | clean |
| sich (*Dat*) die Haare waschen <br> (er wäscht sich...) (*s*) | to wash one's hair |
| das (Haar)shampoo (-s) <br> das Haarwaschmittel (-) } | shampoo |
| der Haartrockner (-) <br> der Fön (-e) ® } | hair-drier |
| sich bürsten | to brush one's hair (*Dat*) |
| die Haarbürste (-n) | hairbrush |
| der Kamm (¨e) | comb |
| sich kämmen | to comb one's hair (*Dat*) |

| sich ausziehen (er zieht sich aus) | |
|---|---|
| (s; sep) | to undress |
| sich anziehen (er zieht sich an) | |
| (s; sep) | to dress |
| ausziehen (er zieht ... aus) | |
| (s; sep) | to take off |
| anziehen (s; sep) | to put on |
| ich ziehe meinen Pullover aus/an | I take off/put on my pullover |
| tragen (s) | to wear |
| sich schminken | to put on make-up |

See also Clothes, pages 136–8 for clothes and Bathroom, pages 74–5 for more bathroom vocabulary.

## Jetzt bist du dran! 4

Was machst du morgens?
Schreib Sätze!

What do you do in the morning? Write sentences.

Beispiel: Ich wache auf.

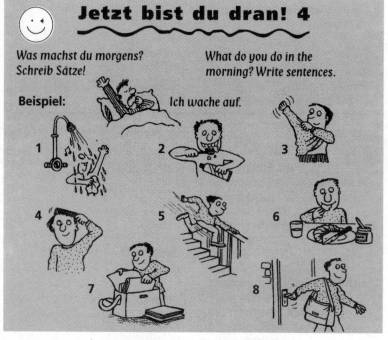

| nach unten gehen* | to go downstairs |
|---|---|
| das Frühstück | breakfast |
| die Küche (-n) | kitchen |
| frühstücken | to have breakfast |
| die Zeitung lesen | to read the newspaper |
| Butterbrote vorbereiten (sep) | to make sandwiches |

See also Food, page 36 and In the kitchen, pages 70–2.

| | |
|---|---|
| **sich fertigmachen** (*sep*) | to get ready |
| **die Schultasche** (-n) | school bag |
| **packen** | to pack |
| **die Schulsachen** (*pl*) | school things |
| **suchen** | to look for, seek |
| **holen** | to fetch |
| **finden** (er findet) (*s*) | to find |

## Jetzt bist du dran! 5

*Wie viele sinnvolle Sätze kannst du bilden?*   *How many sentences that make sense can you form from this grid?*

| | | | | |
|---|---|---|---|---|
| Zuerst | stehe ich | mich | schnell | auf. |
| Wenn ich aufwache, | gehe ich | mir | so schnell wie | ins Bad. |
| Wenn ich aufstehe, | steige ich | | möglich | im Bad. |
| Schon um sieben Uhr | laufe ich | | langsam | nach unten. |
| Gleich danach | wasche ich | | in aller Ruhe | die Treppe hinunter. |
| Dann | bürste ich | | sofort | in die Küche. |
| Kurz nachher | kämme ich | | | in der Küche. |
| Jeden Tag | schminke ich | | | aus dem Bett. |
| Jeden Morgen | esse ich | | | die Haare. |
| Nach fünf Minuten | frühstücke ich | | | |

## b In die Schule gehen

## Going to school

| | |
|---|---|
| **das Haus verlassen** (er verläßt) (*s; insep*) | to leave the house |
| **auf den Bus warten** | to wait for the bus |
| **den Bus erreichen** (*insep*) | to catch the bus |
| **den Bus verpassen** (*insep*) | to miss the bus |
| **zu Fuß gehen\*** (*s*) ⎫ **laufen\*** (er läuft) (*s*) ⎭ | to walk |
| **sich beeilen** (*insep*) | to hurry |
| **mit dem Rad** | by bike |
| **mit dem Zug** | by train |
| **mit dem Bus** | by bus |
| **mit der U-Bahn** | by underground |
| **(mein Vater) bringt mich mit dem Auto in die Schule** | (my father) takes me to school by car |
| **die Fahrt dauert...** | the trip takes... |
| **pünktlich** | on time, punctual(ly) |

| | |
|---|---|
| heute bin ich zu spät gekommen | I was late today |
| in der Schule ankommen* | |
| (er kommt ... an) (s; sep) | to arrive at school |
| Punkt neun Uhr | on the stroke of nine |
| es läutet/klingelt | the bell rings |

## c Nach der Schule — After school

| | |
|---|---|
| der Unterricht ist um 4 Uhr | |
| zu Ende | lessons finish at 4 pm |
| die Schule ist um 4 /16 Uhr aus | school finishes at 4 pm |
| treffen (er trifft) (s) | to meet |
| sich mit den Freunden treffen (s) | to meet one's friends |
| (meine Mutter) holt mich ab | (my mother) fetches me |
| die Arbeitsgemeinschaft (-en) | |
| (die AG) | club |
| die Schach-AG | chess club |
| die Gruppe (-n) | club |
| die Theatergruppe | drama club |
| Sport treiben (er treibt) (s) | to do sport |
| nach Hause gehen* (s) | to go home |

For other leisure activities see also pages 81–95.

## d Abends — Evenings

| | |
|---|---|
| zu Hause sein* | to be at home |
| das Abendessen | |
| das Abendbrot | } supper |
| zu Abend essen (er ißt) (s) | to have supper |
| eine Mahlzeit einnehmen | |
| (er nimmt ... ein) (s; sep) | to eat a meal |
| ich nehme das Abendessen | I have supper at about 6 o'clock |
| gegen sechs Uhr ein | (formal) |
| das Tablett (-e or -s) | tray |
| der Schoß (auf dem Schoß) | lap (on one's lap) |

| | |
|---|---|
| die Hausaufgaben (pl) | homework |
| lernen | to learn, do homework |
| Hausaufgaben machen | to do homework |
| zwei Stunden lang | for two hours |
| wir haben für Englisch etwas auf | } |
| wir haben Englisch auf | } we've got English homework |
| wiederholen (insep) | to revise |

| | |
|---|---|
| üben | to practise |
| einen Aufsatz schreiben (s) | to write an essay |
| fertig | finished, over |

| | |
|---|---|
| sich umziehen (s; sep) | to change clothes |
| Freunde anrufen (s; sep) | to ring friends |
| ausgehen* (er geht aus) (s; sep) | to go out |
| Musik hören | to listen to music |
| fernsehen (er sieht fern) (s; sep) | to watch TV |
| ein Buch ⎫<br>eine Zeitschrift ⎬lesen<br>eine Zeitung ⎭ | ⎧book<br>to read a ⎨magazine<br>⎩newspaper |
| ich räume mein Zimmer auf | I tidy up my room |
| nichts Besonderes tun (er tut) (s) | to do nothing special |
| aufbleiben* (er bleibt auf) (s) | to stay up |
| werktags ⎫<br>wochentags ⎭ | on weekdays |
| ins Bett gehen* (s) ⎫<br>schlafen gehen* (s) ⎭ | to go to bed |
| einschlafen* (er schläft ein)<br>(s; sep) | to go to sleep |
| schlafen (s) | to sleep |
| erst nach einer Stunde | not for an hour |
| erst gegen 23 Uhr | not until about 11 o'clock |
| träumen | to dream |
| der Traum (¨e) | dream |
| der Alptraum (¨e) | nightmare |
| schlaf gut! | sleep well |

*Wie viele sinnvolle Sätze kannst du bilden?*  *How many sentences that make sense can you form from this grid?*

| | | | |
|---|---|---|---|
| Ich stehe | um | sieben Uhr | auf. |
| Ich wasche mich | etwa um | Viertel nach sieben | an. |
| Ich frühstücke | gegen | halb neun | ein. |
| Ich verlasse das Haus | | Viertel vor eins | aus. |
| Die Stunden fangen | | fünf vor zwei | |
| Die Mittagspause fängt | | vier Uhr | |
| Die Schule ist | | halb fünf | |
| Wir essen zu Abend | | Viertel nach sechs | |
| Ich beginne meine Hausaufgaben | | zehn Uhr | |

## e Am Wochenende    At the weekend

| | |
|---|---|
| am Wochende | at the weekend |
| samstags | on Saturdays |
| sonntags | on Sundays |
| frei haben | to have time off |
| die Freizeit | free time/leisure |
| schulfrei haben | to have no school |
| ein schulfreier Samstag | a Saturday without school |

*(Some German schools have lessons on certain Saturdays each month.)*

| | |
|---|---|
| ausschlafen (er schläft aus) (*s; sep*) | to sleep in |
| sich ausruhen (*sep*) <br> sich entspannen (*insep*) | to relax |
| faulenzen | to laze about |
| zu Hause bleiben* (er bleibt) (*s*) | to stay at home |
| ich helfe meinen Eltern | I help my parents |
| (mit dem Computer) spielen | to play (with the computer) |
| Sport treiben (er treibt) (*s*) | to do sport |
| der Job (-s) | job (*Saturdays etc*) |
| eine Teilzeitarbeit | part-time job |
| Geld verdienen | to earn money |
| Zeitungen austragen <br> (er trägt ... aus) (*s; sep*) | to deliver newspapers |
| Einkaufen gehen* (*s*) | to go shopping |

| | |
|---|---|
| die Party (-s) <br> die Fete (-n) | party |
| die Feier (-n) | celebration, party |
| Verwandte besuchen (*insep*) | to visit relations |
| die Disco/Disko/Diskothek | disco |
| tanzen | to dance |
| ins Eiscafé gehen* (*s*) <br> in die Eisdiele gehen* (*s*) | to go to an ice-cream parlour |

| | |
|---|---|
| sonntags morgens | on Sunday mornings |
| in die Kirche gehen* (*s*) | to go to church |
| anglikanisch | Anglican |
| evangelisch | Protestant |
| katholisch | Roman Catholic |
| die Synagoge (-n) | synagogue |
| die Moschee (-n) | mosque |
| der Tempel (-) | temple |

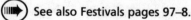 See also Festivals pages 97–8.

### 4 Der Alltag in der Schule

### School routine

*The* du *form is quoted first; the* ihr *form is in square brackets.*

| **a Am Anfang des Tages** | **At the beginning of the day** |
|---|---|
| der Alltag | everyday life |
| guten Tag! | good morning |
| wie geht's? | how are you? |
| die Namensliste | register |
| fehlt jemand? | is anyone absent? |
| wo ist Thomas? | where's Thomas? |
| Thomas ist heute nicht da | Thomas isn't here today |
| er ist krank | he's ill |
| es klingelt | the bell's ringing |

| **b Probleme** | **Problems** |
|---|---|
| warum kommst du [kommt ihr] so spät? | why are you so late? |
| ich habe verschlafen | I overslept |
| der Bus hatte Verspätung | the bus was late |
| es gab einen Stau | there was a traffic jam |
| ich habe mit Frau X gesprochen | I was talking to Mrs X |
| wo sind deine Hausaufgaben | where is your homework |
| es tut mir leid... | I'm sorry... |
| ...ich habe meine Hausaufgaben nicht | ...I haven't got my homework |
| ...ich habe sie nicht fertiggeschrieben | ...I haven't finished it |
| ...ich habe (mein Heft) vergessen | ...I've forgotten (my exercise book) |
| ...ich habe (mein Buch) verloren | ...I've lost (my textbook) |
| ...ich war krank | ...I was ill |
| ...ich war zu müde | ...I was too tired |
| ...ich hatte keine Zeit | ...I didn't have time |
| ...es war zu schwierig | ...it was too difficult |
| ...der Hund hat sie gefressen | ...the dog ate it |
| eine faule Ausrede | a lame excuse |
| Entschuldigung, Herr/Frau X | excuse me, Sir/Miss |
| was ist los? | what's the matter? |
| ich habe ... vergessen | I have forgotten... |

| | |
|---|---|
| ich weiß nicht | I don't know |
| Ich brauche (einen Kuli) | I need (a ballpoint pen) |
| hast du [habt ihr] denn keinen Füller? | haven't you got a fountain pen? |
| ich verstehe nicht | I don't understand |
| noch einmal, bitte | again, please |
| wie bitte? | I beg your pardon |
| welche Seite, Herr/Frau X? | which page, Sir/Miss? |
| wie wird ... geschrieben? | how do you spell...? |
| wie sagt man ... auf Deutsch? | how do you say ... in German? |
| was bedeutet das? | what does that mean? |
| was sollen wir machen? | what do we have to do? |
| ich kann dich [euch] nicht hören | I can't hear you (*informal*) |
| ich kann Sie nicht hören | I can't hear you (*formal*) |
| darf ich bitte auf die Toilette/ aufs Klo gehen? | please may I go to the toilet? |

## c Anweisungen an die Klasse
## Instructions to the class

| | |
|---|---|
| komm [kommt] herein! | come in |
| geh [geht] hinaus! | go out |
| mach [macht] die Tür auf! | open the door |
| mach [macht] die Tür zu! | shut the door |
| setz dich [setzt euch]! | sit down |
| steh [steht] auf! | stand up |
| nimm deine [nehmt eure] Bücher heraus! | get your books out |
| du träumst [ihr träumt] | you're day-dreaming |
| schlag [schlagt] Seite 20 auf! | open your books at page 20 |
| lies [lest] den Text! | read the text |
| beantworte [beantwortet] die Fragen! | answer the questions |
| sieh [seht] auf die Tafel! | look at the board |
| öffne [öffnet] das Fenster! | open the window |
| mach [macht] das Licht an! | turn on the light |
| mach [macht] das Licht aus! | turn off the light |
| arbeitet mit euren Partnern/ euren Partnerinnen! | work with your partners |

## d Mündliche Übungen
## Oral and listening practice

| | |
|---|---|
| sag [sagt] es auf deutsch! | say it in German |
| lies [lest] bitte vor! | please read out loud |

| | |
|---|---|
| lauter | more loudly |
| leiser | more quietly |
| sprich [sprecht] deutlicher! | speak more clearly |
| langsam | slowly |

| | |
|---|---|
| bespreche [besprecht]! | discuss |
| erkläre [erklärt]! | explain |
| stell [stellt] Fragen! | ask questions |
| beantworte [beantwortet] die Fragen! | answer the questions |
| buchstabiere [buchstabiert]! | spell it |
| wiederhole [wiederholt] das! | repeat that |

| | |
|---|---|
| hör dir [hört euch] die Kassette an! | listen to the cassette |
| hör [hört] genau/aufmerksam zu! | listen carefully |
| du hörst [ihr hört] ein Gespräch über... | you will hear a conversation about... |

| | |
|---|---|
| jeder einzeln | one at a time |
| alle zusammen | all together |

## e Übungen an der Tafel          Board exercises

| | |
|---|---|
| sich (Dat) etwas ansehen (er sieht ... an) (s; sep) / sich etwas anschauen (sep) | to look at |
| seht/schaut euch dieses Bild an! | look at this picture |
| schau [schaut] auf die Tafel! | look at the board |
| schreib [schreibt] das an die Tafel! | write that on the board |
| streich [streicht] das durch! | cross that out |
| wisch [wischt] das aus! | wipe that off |
| putz [putzt] die Tafel! | wipe the board |
| nimm [nehmt] die Kreide! | take the chalk |
| schreib [schreibt] größer! | write larger |

## f Schriftliche Übungen          Written exercises

| | |
|---|---|
| schreib deinen [schreibt eure] Namen! | write your name |
| folge [folgt] den Anweisungen! | follow the instructions |
| mach [macht] die Übung! | do the exercise |
| schreib [schreibt] das auf! | write that down |

| | |
|---|---|
| fang [fangt] an! | begin |
| mach [macht] weiter! | carry on |
| bist du [seid ihr] schon fertig? | have you finished yet? |
| hör [hört] auf! | stop now |
| leg deinen [legt eure] Füller hin! | put down your pen(s) |
| schließ deine [schließt eure] Bücher! | close your books |
| geh [geht] die Übung noch mal durch! | check your work |
| zeig mir deine [zeigt mir eure] Arbeit! | show me your work |
| bring dein Buch [bringt eure Bücher] her! | bring your book(s) here |

| | |
|---|---|
| ordentlich | neatly |
| Vorsicht! } Achtung! } | careful |
| verstehst du? [versteht ihr?] | do you understand? |
| hat jemand Fragen? | any questions? |
| hier ist ein Beispiel | here is an example |

| | |
|---|---|
| wir machen Übung zwei | we'll do exercise two |
| schreib [schreibt] den Brief an Paul! | write the letter to Paul |
| erzähle [erzählt] von der Reise! | talk about the journey |

schreib [schreibt] { einen Bericht (-e) über...! — write a report } on...
{ eine Zusammenfassung (-en) — summary }
{ einen Artikel (-) — article }

| | |
|---|---|
| das Diagramm (-e) | diagram |
| der Fragebogen (¨) | questionnaire |
| bitte umblättern! | please turn over |

| | |
|---|---|
| zeichne [zeichnet] (ein Auto)! | draw (a car) |
| beschrifte [beschriftet] die Zeichnung! | label the drawing |
| schneide [schneidet] ... aus! | cut out... |
| füll [füllt] die Lücken aus! | fill in the gaps |
| ordne [ordnet] diese Sätze! | put these sentences in order |
| durchstreichen (er streicht ... durch) (s; sep) | to cross out |
| unterstreichen (er unterstreicht) (s; insep) | to underline |
| richtig oder falsch? | true or false? |

| | |
|---|---|
| hake [hakt] die richtige Antwort ab! | tick the correct answer |
| der Haken (-) | tick |
| das Kreuz (-e) | cross |
| kreuze [kreuzt] das Feld an! | put a cross in the box |
| schreib [schreibt] den entsprechenden Buchstaben ins Heft! | write the corresponding letter in your book(s) |
| | |
| du wirst [ihr werdet] nicht alle Buchstaben brauchen | you will not need all the letters |
| bitte in Blockschrift schreiben! | please write in capital letters |
| ergänze [ergänzt] die Tabelle! | complete the table |
| umkreise [umkreist] das richtige Wort! | circle the correct word |
| sortiere [sortiert] die Wörter zu Wortpaaren! | match up the words in pairs |

 For instructions you are likely to encounter in your exam, see pages 184–6.

## g Ordung — Order

| | |
|---|---|
| Ruhe/ruhig | quiet |
| hör [hört] auf zu sprechen! | stop talking |
| mach [macht] nicht so viel Lärm! | don't make so much noise |
| paß [paßt] auf! | pay attention |
| beeil dich doch [beeilt euch doch]! | do hurry up |
| schnell | quickly |
| sei [seid] nicht albern! | don't be silly |
| drängele [drängelt] nicht so! | don't push like that |
| spiel [spielt] nicht so herum! | don't play about like that |
| dreh dich um [dreht euch um]! | turn round |
| komm mal her! | come here |
| setz dich [setzt euch] hier vorne hin! | come and sit at the front |
| geh [geht] sofort zum Schulleiter! | go to the headmaster straight away |
| strafen | to punish |
| die Strafe (-n) | punishment |

## h Schularten — Types of school

| | |
|---|---|
| besuchen (*insep*) | to attend |
| der Kindergarten (-) | nursery school |
| die Grundschule (-n) | primary school |

| die Gesamtschule (-n) | comprehensive school |
| die Hauptschule (-n) | secondary modern school |
| die Realschule (-n) | intermediate school |
| das Gymnasium (-ien) | grammar school |
| die Hochschule (-n) | college/university |
| die Universität (-en) | university |
| die Klosterschule | convent |
| das Internat (-e) | boarding school |
| der/die Interne (-n) | boarder |
| der/die Externe (-n) | day pupil |
| die Privatschule (-n) | private school |

## i Jahrgänge — Year groups

| erste Klasse | Year 2 (*age 6/7: England*) |
| zweite Klasse | Year 3 (*age 7/8*) |
| dritte Klasse | Year 4 (*age 8/9*) |
| vierte Klasse | Year 5 (*age 9/10*) |
| fünfte Klasse | Year 6 (*age 10/11*) |
| sechste Klasse | Year 7 (*age 11/12*) |
| siebte Klasse | Year 8 (*age 12/13*) |
| achte Klasse | Year 9 (*age 13/14*) |
| neunte Klasse | Year 10 (*age 14/15*) |
| zehnte Klasse | Year 11 (*age 15/16*) |
| die Oberstufe (Klasse 11–13) | Sixth Form |
| Jahrgangsstufe elf | lower sixth |
| Jahrgangsstufe zwölf | upper sixth |
| Jahrgangsstufe dreizehn | (*age 18/19*) |

## j die Gebäude — Premises

| das Gebäude (-) | building |
| das Klassenzimmer (-) | classroom |
| das Labor (-s) | lab |
| das Laboratorium (-ien) | laboratory |
| das Sprachlabor (-s) | language lab |
| die Kabine (-n) | booth |
| der Werkraum (-̈e) | workshop |
| das Lehrerzimmer (-) | staff room |
| die Aula (Aulen) | assembly hall |
| die Bibliothek (-en) | library |
| der Speisesaal (-säle) | dining hall |
| das Krankenzimmer (-) | sick bay |
| die Turnhalle (-n) | gymnasium |

| | |
|---|---|
| **der Sportplatz (¨e)** | sports ground |
| **das Schwimmbad (¨er)** | swimming pool |
| **der Hof/Schulhof (¨e)** | playground |
| **die Kantine** | canteen |
| **der Speisesaal (-säle)** | dining hall |
| **anstehen\* (er steht … an)** | |
| **(s; *sep*)** | to queue up |
| **sich anstellen (*sep*)** | to queue up |
| **die Schlange (-n)** | queue |
| **sich vordrängen (*sep*)** | to push in |
| **die Portion (-en)** | helping |
| **man kann noch etwas nachbekommen** | |
| **(er bekommt … nach)(*s; sep*)** | you can get seconds |
| **ein Lehrer hat Aufsicht** | a teacher is on duty |
| **aufräumen (*sep*)** | to clear away |
| **die Garderobe (-n)** | cloakroom |

# Jetzt bist du dran! 7

*Wähl die richtigen Zeichen für die Schulgebäude aus!*

*Match up the symbols with the parts of the school.*

**Beispiel:**  = *der Sportplatz*

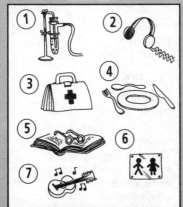

(1) (2) (3) (4) (5) (6) (7)

(a) die Bibliothek
(b) die Toiletten
(c) das Laboratorium
(d) **das Musikzimmer**
(e) das Sprachlabor
(f) *die Kantine*
(g) das Krankenzimmer

## k Die Ausstattung — School equipment

| | |
|---|---|
| die Ausstattung | equipment |
| der Tisch (-e) | desk, table |
| das Pult (-e) | school desk |
| der Arbeitstisch (-e) | desk, workbench |
| die Tafel (-n) | blackboard, whiteboard |
| die Kreide | chalk |
| der Filzschreiber (-) | board-marker |
| der Lappen (-) | board-wiper, cloth |
| der Schwamm (¨e) | sponge |
| der Tageslichtprojektor | overhead projector |
| die Folie (-n) | OHP transparency |
| die Bank (¨e) | bench |
| das Schreibmaterial | stationery |
| der Bleistift (-e) | pencil |
| der Stift (-e) | pencil/pen |
| der Radierer/Radiergummi (-s) | rubber |
| der Filzstift (-e) | felt-tip pen |
| der Kugelschreiber (-) | ball-point pen |
| der Kuli (-s) | biro, ball-point |
| der Füller (-) | fountain pen |
| die Tinte | ink |
| die Patrone (-n) | cartridge |
| die Korrekturflüssigkeit | correction fluid |
| das Lineal (-e) | ruler |
| gerade | straight |
| der/das Zentimeter (-) (cm) | centimetre (cm) |
| das Federmäppchen (-) } das Etui (-s) } | pencil-case |
| der Taschenrechner (-) | calculator |
| der Computer (-) | computer |
| das Heft (-e) | exercise-book |
| das Ringbuch (¨er) } der Hefter (-) } | ring binder |
| der Ordner | lever arch file |
| das Papier | paper |
| das Buch (¨er) | book |
| das Schulbuch (¨er) | textbook |
| das Klassenbuch (¨er) | class register |
| das Blatt (¨er) | sheet of paper |
| der Zettel (-) | note, piece of paper |
| die Schultasche (-n) | schoolbag |
| die Mappe (-n) | briefcase, schoolbag |

**die Aktentasche (-n)** briefcase

 See also Computers and IT, pages 168–70.

---

## Jetzt bist du dran! 8

*Verbinde die Wörter, die zusammenpassen!*

*Join up the words that belong together*

*das Pult*
*die Bank*
*die Federballnetze*
*die Mäntel*
*das Geschirr*
*die Umkleidekabinen*

*die Turnhalle*
*das Labor*
*das Klassenzimmer*
*der Speisesaal*
*die Garderobe*
*das Schwimmbad*

---

## l Leute    People

| male | female | definition |
|---|---|---|
| der Schulleiter (-) | die Schulleiterin (-nen) | headteacher |
| der Direktor (-en) | die Direktorin (-nen) | headteacher (*at* Gymnasium) |
| der Klassenlehrer (-) | die Klassenlehrerin (-nen) | class teacher |
| der Lehrer (-) | die Lehrerin (-nen) | teacher |
| der Klassensprecher (-) | die Klassensprecherin (-nen) | class rep (*approx*) |
| der Hausmeister (-) | die Hausmeisterin (-nen) | caretaker |
| der Schüler (-) | die Schülerin (-nen) | pupil |
| der Student (-en) | die Studentin (-nen) | student (university, college) |
| der Schulfreund (-e) | die Schulfreundin (-nen) | schoolfriend |

**der Schülerlotse (-n, -n)**    (pupil acting as) road crossing warden

## m Die Lehrer beschreiben    Describing teachers

| | |
|---|---|
| **fördert das Selbstbewußtsein** | inspires confidence |
| **unterrichtet gut** | teaches well |
| **gibt deutliche Erklärungen** | explains clearly |
| **macht den Unterricht interessant** | makes the work interesting |
| **ist gut/schlecht organisiert** | is well/badly organised |
| **freundlich** | friendly |

| | |
|---|---|
| **nett** | nice |
| **sympathisch** | kind |
| **hilfsbereit** | helpful |
| **helfen (+Dat) (s)** | to help |
| **begeistert** | enthusiastic |
| **gleichgültig** | indifferent |
| **locker** | relaxed |
| **nervös** | nervous |
| **amüsant** | amusing |
| **langweilig** | boring |
| **begabt** | gifted |
| **nutzlos** | useless |
| **geduldig** | patient |
| **ungeduldig** | impatient |
| **streng** | strict |
| **anspruchsvoll** | demanding |
| **anspruchslos** | undemanding |

# Jetzt bist du dran! 9

Beschreib deine Lehrer. Hier sind mögliche Antworten:

Describe your teachers. Here are some possible answers:

| | | | |
|---|---|---|---|
| Mein(e) Mathelehrer(in) ist | immer | sehr | jung/alt (etwa wie alt?). |
| Mein(e) Französischlehrer(in) ist | manchmal | ziemlich | interessant/langweilig. |
| Mein(e) Geschichtslehrer(in) ist | oft | ein wenig | in der Schule/krank. |
| Mein(e) Geographielehrer(in) ist | nie | ganz | streng/gar nicht streng. |
| Mein(e) Deutschlehrer(in) ist | normaler- weise | wirklich | sportlich/dick. |
| Mein(e) Chemielehrer(in) ist | beinahe immer | echt | gut gelaunt/schlecht gelaunt. |
| Mein(e) Biolehrer(in) ist | leider | | gut/schlecht. |
| Mein(e) Physiklehrer(in) ist | zum Glück | | sympathisch/böse. |
| Mein(e) Sportlehrer(in) ist | ab und zu | | freundlich/zornig. |
| Mein(e) Kunstlehrer(in) ist | in der Regel | | geduldig/ungeduldig. |
| Mein(e) Religionlehrer(in) ist | jeden Tag | | pünktlich/verspätet. |
| Mein(e) Englischlehrer(in) ist | regelmäßig | | lustig/ernst. |
| Mein(e) Lateinlehrer(in) ist | selten | | intelligent/unintelligent. |
| Mein(e) Klassenlehrer(in) ist | | | fleißig/faul. |
| Mein(e) Schulleiter(in) ist | | | schüchtern/laut. |

## n Der Stundenplan — Timetable

|  |  |
|---|---|
| das Schuljahr (-e) | school year |
| der Schulanfang (-e) | beginning of term |
| die Namen ausrufen | to take the register |
| die Morgenandacht (-en) | assembly |
| das Trimester (-) | term (*British*) |
| der Stundenplan (-e) | timetable |
| die Ganztagsschule | all-day schooling |
| die Halbtagsschule | half-day schooling |
| die Pause (-n) | break |
| die Morgenpause (-n) | morning break |
| die Mittagspause (-n) | lunch break |
| schreiben (er schreibt) (*s*) | to write |
| die Schrift (-en) | handwriting |
| lesen (er liest) (*s*) | to read |
| das Lesen | reading |
| die Aufgabe (-n) | exercise |
| das Beispiel (-e) | example |
| der Fehler (-) | mistake |
| der Lehrplan (-e) | syllabus |
| das Fach (-er) | subject |
| das Lieblingsfach (-er) | favourite subject |
| das Pflichtfach (-er) | compulsory subject |
| das Wahlfach (-er) | optional subject |
| das Hauptfach (-er) | main subject |
| das Nebenfach (-er) | subsidiary subject |
| die beiden Fächer | both subjects |
| (die) Mathematik / Mathe | mathematics |
| (das) Rechnen | arithmetic |
| der Taschenrechner (-) | (pocket) calculator |
| der Computer (-) | computer |
| (die) Computerlehre / (die) Informatik | computer studies/IT |
| (die) Elektronik | electronics |
| (die) Technik | technology |
| (die) Naturwissenschaften (*pl*) | sciences |
| (die) Physik | physics |
| (die) Chemie | chemistry |

| | |
|---|---|
| **(die) Biologie** | biology |
| **die Fremdsprache (-n)** | foreign language |
| **die alten Sprachen** | classics (*Latin & Greek*) |
| **die neueren Sprachen** | modern languages |
| **(das) Englisch** | English |
| **(das) Deutsch** | German |
| **(das) Französisch** | French |
| **(das) Spanisch** | Spanish |
| **(das) Italienisch** | Italian |
| **(das) Russisch** | Russian |
| **(das) Latein** | Latin |
| **(das) Griechisch** | Greek |
| **übersetzen** | to translate |
| **fließend sprechen (er spricht) (s)** | to speak fluently |
| **der Satz (¨e)** | sentence |
| **der Ausdruck (¨e)** | expression |
| **die Grammatik** | grammar |
| **(die) Erdkunde** / **(die) Geographie** | geography |
| **(die) Geschichte** | history |
| **(die) Sozialkunde** | social studies |
| **(die) Wirtschaftslehre** | business studies |
| **die Wirtschaftswissenschaften (*pl*)** | economics |
| **(die) Religion** | religious studies |
| **(das) Maschineschreiben** | typing |
| **(die) Kunst** | art |
| **(die) Handarbeit** | needlework |
| **(das) Schreinern** | woodwork |
| **(die) Metallarbeit** | metalwork |
| **(das) Werken** | CDT, handicrafts |
| **Technisches Zeichnen** | technical drawing |
| **(das) Töpfern** | pottery |
| **die Hauswirtschaft/ Hauswirtschaftslehre** | domestic science |
| **das Nähen** | sewing |
| **(das) Kochen** | cookery |
| **(der) Sportunterricht** | physical education |

## Jetzt bist du dran! 10

| Wie viele sinnvolle Sätze kannst du bilden? | | | How many true sentences can you make? | |
|---|---|---|---|---|
| Wenn ich ankomme, | plaudere ich | manchmal | im Klassenzimmer | mit den Freunden. |
| Sofort | gehe ich | ab und zu | in die Aula | mit den Freundinnen. |
| Noch vor der Schule | finde ich | vielleicht | in der Aula | meine Butterbrote. |
| In der Pause | kaufe ich | normalerweise | auf den Schulhof | mein zweites Frühstück. |
| In der Mittagspause | esse ich | fast jeden Tag | auf dem Schulhof | Süßigkeiten. |
| Zwischen den Stunden | trinke ich | oft | im Korridor | eine Cola. |
| Wenn es klingelt, | höre ich | | im Schulladen | Musik. |

| o Der Unterricht | Lessons |
|---|---|
| die Stunde (-n) | lesson |
| unterrichten | to teach |
| ausfallen* (er fällt aus) (s; sep) | to be cancelled |
| der Stundenplan (¨e) | timetable |
| dauern | to last |
| die Hausaufgaben (pl) | homework |
| der Aufsatz (¨e) | essay |
| das Beispiel (-e) | example |
| zum Beispiel (z.B.) | for example (eg) |
| eine Frage stellen | to ask a question |
| die Antwort (-en) | answer |
| antworten | to answer (intransitive) |
| antworten auf (+Acc) | to respond to |
| er hat richtig geantwortet | he answered correctly |
| beantworten (insep) | to answer (transitive) |
| er hat die Frage beantwortet | he answered the question |
| lesen (er liest) (s) | to read |
| aufpassen (sep) | to pay attention to |
| zuhören (+Dat) (sep) | to listen (to) |
| erfahren (er erfährt) (s; insep) | to discover, learn |
| rechnen | to calculate, do sums |

| | |
|---|---|
| **lernen** | to learn, do homework, to study |
| **loben** | to praise |
| **korrigieren** | to correct, mark |
| **die Note (-n)** | mark, grade |
| **der Fehler (-)** | mistake |
| **vergessen (er vergißt) *(s; insep)*** | to forget |
| **abschreiben (er schreibt ... ab) *(s; sep)*** | to copy (*allowed or not*) |
| **kopieren** | to copy out |
| **mogeln** | to cheat |
| **fehlen** | to be absent |
| **schwänzen** | to play truant, skive |
| **verpassen *(insep)*** | to miss (*eg a lesson*) |
| **zu spät kommen (er kommt) *(s)*** | to be late |
| **pünktlich** | on time, punctual(ly) |
| **die Strafarbeit (-en)** | punishment, imposition |
| **bestrafen *(insep)*** | to punish |
| **nachsitzen (er sitzt nach) *(s; sep)*** | to be kept in detention |
| **hitzefrei haben** | to have time off school because of the heat |
| **das (Schul)halbjahr (-)** | term (*half the school year*) |
| **das Trimester (-)** | term (*a third of British school year*) |
| **die Klassenfahrt (-en)** | class trip |

# Jetzt bist du dran! 11

Bilde Sätze über das, was du in der Schule machst.

Construct sentences about what you do in school.

| Was? | Wann? Wie lange? | Wo? | |
|---|---|---|---|
| Ich lerne | jeden Tag | in der Schule | Sport, Hockey usw. |
| Ich spiele | fast/beinahe jeden Tag | im Klassenzimmer | die neueren Sprachen. |
| Ich arbeite | jeden Vormittag | im Laboratorium | Deutsch, Französisch. |
| Ich treibe | dreimal in der Woche | im Sprachlabor | Physik, Chemie, |
| Wir haben | eine halbe Stunde lang | auf dem Sportplatz | Biologie. |
| Wir bekommen | vierzig Minuten lang | in der Turnhalle | Werken. |
| | viel zu oft | im Hallenbad | Informatik. |
| | | in den Werkstätten | Religion. |
| | | | Englisch. |

## p Der Fortschritt — Progress

| | |
|---|---|
| der Fortschritt (-e) | progress |
| gern haben | to like |
| ich habe Mathe gern | I like maths |
| vorziehen (er zieht … vor) (s; sep) | to prefer |
| sich anstrengen (sep) | to try hard |
| wählen | to choose |
| (nicht) besonders gut in… | (not) especially good in… |
| Geschichte kann ich überhaupt nicht | I'm no good at history |
| auch | also, too |
| sowie | as well as |
| sowohl X als auch Y | both X and Y |

| | |
|---|---|
| (un)wichtig | (un)important |
| leicht | easy |
| schwer / schwierig | difficult |
| kompliziert | complicated |
| interessant | interesting |
| langweilig | boring |
| aufregend | exciting |
| zwecklos | pointless |
| die Verbesserung (-en) | improvement |

| | |
|---|---|
| können (er kann) (s) | to be able to, to know |
| ich kann Deutsch | I can speak German |
| auswendig lernen | to learn by heart |
| einen Fehler machen / sich vertun | to make a mistake |
| ich habe mich vertan | I have made a mistake |
| korrigieren | to correct |

## q Prüfungen — Exams

| | |
|---|---|
| wiederholen (insep) | to revise/repeat |
| pauken | to swot, cram |
| lernen | to learn, study |
| die Nachhilfe | extra help, private tuition |
| mogeln | to cheat |
| die Prüfung (-en) | test, exam |
| die Klassenarbeit (-en) | regular major test (several per year) |

| | |
|---|---|
| die Klausur (-en) | regular major test (*for senior pupils/at University*) |
| das Examen (Examina) | (*major*) examination |
| mündlich | oral |
| schriftlich | written |
| eine Prüfung ablegen (*sep*) | to sit an exam |
| eine Arbeit schreiben | to do a test |
| (eine Prüfung) machen | to do, sit (*an exam*) |
| bestehen (er besteht) (*s; insep*) | to pass |
| durchfallen* (er fällt ... durch) (*s; sep*) | to fail |
| die Stufe (-n) | level |
| die mittlere Reife | equivalent to GCSE |
| das Abitur | equivalent to A level |
| der Abiturient/die Abiturientin | person doing/who has done Abitur (*m/f*) |
| die Abschlußprüfung (-en) | school leaving exam(s) |

# Jetzt bist du dran! 12

Wie findest du deine Fächer in der Schule?

What do you think of the subjects you learn?

| Englisch: | Das ist | ein Kinderspiel! |
|---|---|---|
| Französisch: | Das wird | sehr leicht. |
| Deutsch: | | nicht zu kompliziert. |
| Spanisch: | | gar nicht schwer. |
| Latein: | | schon etwas schwer. |
| Mathe: | | manchmal etwas schwer. |
| Physik: | | mein Lieblingsfach! |
| Chemie: | | schon etwas langweilig. |
| Bio: | | immer schwerer. |
| Geschichte: | | unmöglich. |
| Geographie: | | total uninteressant. |
| Religion: | | mein schlechtestes Fach. |
| Informatik: | Das lerne ich nicht! | |
| Turnen: | Ich komme da überhaupt nicht mit! | |
| Werken: | Das habe ich wirklich gern. | |
| Sport: | Da muß ich mich wirklich anstrengen. | |

| r Die Noten und Bermerkungen | Marks and comments |
|---|---|
| das Ergebnis (-se) | result |
| 60 Prozent | 60 per cent |
| die Note (-n) | mark, grade |
| 1: sehr gut | very good |
| 2: gut | good |
| 3: befriedigend | satisfactory |
| 4: ausreichend | acceptable |
| 5: mangelhaft | deficient |
| 6: ungenügend | unsatisfactory |
| schlecht | bad |
| schaffen | to manage, achieve |
| er hat eine Zwei geschafft | he managed a grade 2 |
| bestehen (er besteht) (s; *insep*) | to pass |
| der Erfolg | success |
| erfolgreich | successful |
| die Leistung (-en) | achievement |
| ausreichen (*sep*) | to be sufficient |
| durchfallen (er fällt durch) (s; *sep*) | to fail |
| das Zeugnis (-se) | report, certificate |
| eine Eins (-en) | top grade, an A |
| eine Sechs (-en) | bottom grade |
| eine Eins schreiben (er schreibt) (s) | to get an A grade |
| 12 von 20 | 12 out of 20 |

| | |
|---|---|
| versetzt werden*(s) | to be moved up a class |
| sitzenbleiben* (er bleibt sitzen) (s; *sep*) | to have to repeat a year |
| der Fortschritt (-e) | progress |
| gut in Deutsch sein* | to be good at German |
| mittelmäßig in Chemie sein* | to be average at chemistry |
| schwach in Geschichte sein* | to be weak at history |
| hoffnungslos | hopeless |

 See also Exams, pages 31–2.

## Jetzt bist du dran! 13

Finde die Lösungen zu diesen
Fragen. Die Anfangsbuchstaben
ergeben zwei Wörter, die etwas
Schönes bedeuten.

*Fill in the gaps. The initials
make two words which
indicate something pleasant.*

| | |
|---|---|
| __ eine _____ : | Die bestmögliche Note/eine Nummer. |
| __ der _____ : | Das Zimmer, in dem man ißt. |
| __ das _____: | Das Buch mit den Details von den |
| Stunden und den Schülern. | |
| __ das _____: | Das ist für dich Deutsch, natürlich! |
| __ die _____: | Alles über den Computer. |
| __ das _____: | Eine der Stunden, die weniger wichtig sind. |
| __ die _____: | Dort, wo man die Mäntel aufhängt. |
| __ die _____: | Über die Erde und die Menschen. |
| __ das _____: | Dort, wo man Naturwissenschaften lernt. |
| __ der _____: | Gerät zum Multiplizieren. |

## ④ Essen und trinken    Eating and drinking

### a Die Mahlzeiten    Meals

| | |
|---|---|
| das Essen | food |
| das Getränk (-e) | drink |
| Hunger haben | to be hungry |
| hungrig sein | to be hungry |
| essen (er ißt) (s) | to eat |
| Durst haben | to be thirsty |
| durstig | thirsty |
| trinken (er trinkt) (s) | to drink |

| | |
|---|---|
| bei Tisch | at table |
| die Mahlzeit (-en) | meal |

| | |
|---|---|
| das Frühstück | breakfast |
| zum Frühstück | for breakfast |
| das zweite Frühstück | elevenses |

| | |
|---|---|
| das Mittagessen | midday meal, lunch |
| Kaffee und Kuchen | afternoon tea (*approx*) |
| das Abendbrot | supper |
| das Abendessen | evening meal, supper |
| zu Abend essen | to have supper |
| der Imbiß (Imbisse) | snack |
| das Gericht (-e) | dish (*type of food*) |
| die Vorspeise (-n) | hors d'œuvre, starter |
| das Hauptgericht (-e) | main dish, main course |
| der Nachtisch (-e) }<br>die Nachspeise (-n) } | dessert, sweet |

| | |
|---|---|
| guten Appetit! | enjoy your meal! |
| danke, gleichfalls | thanks, the same to you |
| hat's geschmeckt? | did you enjoy it? |
| servieren | to serve |
| kriegen | to get (*colloquial*) |
| ein wenig | a little |
| leer | empty |
| voll | full (*plate, container, etc*) |

| | |
|---|---|
| beißen (er beißt) (s) | to bite |
| kauen | to chew |
| genügen | to be enough |
| das genügt danke, ich bin schon satt | that's enough, thank you, I'm full up |
| sich satt essen | to eat one's fill |
| die Kartoffeln sind schon alle | the potatoes are all finished |
| das reicht | that's enough |

## b Besteck und Geschirr — Cutlery and crockery

| | |
|---|---|
| das Besteck | cutlery |
| der Löffel (-) | spoon |
| der Teelöffel (-) | teaspoon |
| der Eßlöffel (-) | dessert spoon |
| die Gabel (-n) | fork |
| das Messer (-) | knife |

| | |
|---|---|
| das Geschirr | crockery, kitchenware |
| fallenlassen (er läßt ... fallen) (s) | to drop |
| aus Versehen | by accident |
| das Glas (¨er) | glass, jar |
| die Tasse (-n) | cup |

| die Untertasse (-n) | saucer |
|---|---|
| der Teller (-) | plate |
| die Schüssel (-n) | dish, bowl |

See also In the kitchen, pages 70–2.

## c Das Essen — Food

| schmecken | to taste |
|---|---|
| mir schmeckt es | I like it |
| der Geschmack (-̈e) | taste |
| lecker } köstlich | tasty, delicious |
| süß | sweet |
| gezuckert | sweetened, sugared |
| saftig | juicy |
| salzig | salty |
| knusprig | crisp, crunchy |
| fett | fatty |
| sauer | sour |
| bitter | bitter |
| scharf | hot, spicy |
| gewürzt | seasoned |
| kräftig | savoury |
| zäh | tough |
| schlecht | bad |
| furchtbar | awful |
| schrecklich | terrible |
| gemischt | mixed |
| unappetitlich | unappetising |
| (un)gesund | (un)healthy |

| vorbereiten (*sep*) | to prepare |
|---|---|
| braten (er brät) (*s*) | to roast/fry |
| backen (er backt) (*irreg*) | to bake |

## d Das Frühstück — Breakfast

| das Ei (-er) | egg |
|---|---|
| das hart-/weichgekochte Ei | hard/soft boiled egg |
| das Rührei | scrambled egg |
| das Spiegelei | fried egg |
| pochiertes Ei | poached egg |
| das Omelett (-e) | omelette |

| | |
|---|---|
| der **Käse** | cheese |
| die **Milch** | milk |
| eine **Packung Milch** | a carton of milk |
| die **Vollmilch** | full-cream milk |
| die **fettarme Milch** | semi-skimmed milk |
| die **Magermilch** | skimmed milk |
| der **Joghurt** | yoghurt |
| der **Quark** | soft curd cheese |
| der **Becher (-)** | tub |

| | |
|---|---|
| die **Butter** | butter |
| die **Margarine** | margarine |
| die **Konfitüre** ⎫ die **Marmelade** ⎬ | jam |
| die **Orangenmarmelade** | marmalade |
| der **Honig/Bienenhonig** | honey |
| **streichen (er streicht) (s)** ⎫ **schmieren** ⎬ | to spread |

| | |
|---|---|
| das **Brot (-e)** | bread, loaf |
| das **belegte Brot** | (open) sandwich |
| das **Butterbrot (-e)** | sandwich, slice of bread and butter |
| das **Käsebrot (-e)** | cheese sandwich |
| das **Schinkenbrot (-e)** | ham sandwich |
| das **Vollkornbrot** | wholemeal bread |
| das **Schwarzbrot** | brown bread/German black bread |
| das **Graubrot** | bread made from more than 1 kind of flour |
| das **Brötchen (-)** ⎫ die **Semmel (-n)** ⎬ | bread roll |

| | |
|---|---|
| der **Toast** | toast |
| das **Müsli** | muesli |
| die **Corn-flakes** | corn flakes |

## e Die Lebensmittel — Groceries

| | |
|---|---|
| das **Mehl** | flour |
| der **Zucker** | sugar |
| das **Salz** | salt |
| der **Pfeffer** | pepper |
| der **Senf** | mustard |

| | |
|---|---|
| **der Essig** | vinegar |
| **das Öl** | oil |
| **das Olivenöl** | olive oil |
| **die Chips/Kartoffelchips (*pl*)** | crisps |
| **der Knödel (-)** | dumpling |
| **der Reis** | rice |
| **die Nudeln** | pasta |
| **die Zutaten (*pl*)** | ingredients |

## f Die Konserven — Tinned food

| | |
|---|---|
| **die Dose (-n)** | tin |
| **die Flasche (-n)** | bottle |
| **die Suppe (-n)** | soup |
| **die Tomatensuppe** | tomato soup |
| **die Ochsenschwanzsuppe** | oxtail soup |
| **die Hühnerbrühe** | chicken broth |
| **der Eintopf** | stew |
| **der Gulasch** | goulash (Hungarian stew) |

## g Die Gemüse — Vegetables

| | |
|---|---|
| **das Gemüse (-)** | vegetable(s) |
| **die Kartoffel (-n)** | potato |
| **die Salzkartoffeln (*pl*)** | boiled potatoes |
| **die Bratkartoffeln (*pl*)** | roast potatoes |
| **das Kartoffelpüree** / **der Kartoffelbrei** | mashed potatoes |
| **der Kartoffelsalat** | potato salad |
| **die Pommes frites (*pl*) (Pommes)** | chips |
| **der Kohl** | cabbage |
| **der Rotkohl** | red cabbage |
| **der Blumenkohl** | cauliflower |
| **der Rosenkohl** | Brussels sprouts |
| **das Sauerkraut** | sauerkraut |
| **der Kopfsalat** | lettuce |
| **die Gurke (-n)** | cucumber/gherkin |
| **die Karotte (-n)** / **die Möhre (-n)** | carrot |
| **die Erbse (-n)** | pea |
| **die Bohne (-n)** | bean |
| **die grüne Bohne** | green/French/runner bean |
| **die weiße Bohne** | haricot bean |

| | |
|---|---|
| die Zwiebel (-n) | onion |
| der Knoblauch | garlic |
| der Champignon (-s) | (button) mushroom |
| der (eßbare) Pilz (-e) | mushroom |
| der Spinat | spinach |
| die Zucchini (-) | courgette |
| der Paprika | pepper (*vegetable*) |
| die rote Beete | beetroot |
| der Lauch | leek |

## h Das Obst — Fruit

| | |
|---|---|
| das Obst (*no pl*) }<br>die Frucht (¨e) } | fruit |
| die Tomate (-n) | tomato |
| der Apfel (¨) | apple |
| das Apfelmus | apple purée, apple sauce |
| die Apfelsine (-n) }<br>die Orange (-n) } | orange |
| die Birne (-n) | pear |
| der Pfirsich (-e) | peach |
| die Aprikose (-n) | apricot |
| die Pflaume (-n) | plum |
| die Ananas (-) | pineapple |
| die Grapefruit (-s) | grapefruit |
| die Kirsche (-n) | cherry |
| die Traube/Weintraube (-n) | grape |
| die Beere (-n) | berry |
| die Erdbeere (-n) | strawberry |
| die Himbeere (-n) | raspberry |
| die Brombeere (-n) | blackberry |
| die rote Johannisbeere (-n) | redcurrant |
| die schwarze Johannisbeere (-n) | blackcurrant |
| die Stachelbeere (-n) | gooseberry |
| die Zitrone (-n) | lemon |
| die Limone (-n) | lime |
| die Banane (-n) | banana |
| die Nuß (Nüsse) | nut |
| die Erdnuß (Erdnüsse) | peanut |
| die Schale (-n) | peel, skin |
| das Kompott | stewed fruit |
| pflücken | to pick |

| i Fleisch und Fisch | Meat and fish |
|---|---|
| das Rind(fleisch) | beef |
| das Steak (-s) | steak |
| das Kalbfleisch | veal |
| das Schwein(efleisch) | pork |
| das Kotelett (-e) | chop, cutlet |
| der gekochte Schinken | ham |
| der Früstücksschinken | bacon |
| das Lammfleisch | lamb |
| das Geflügel | poultry |
| das Huhn }<br>das Hähnchen } | chicken |
| die Gans | goose |
| der Puter/die Pute | turkey |
| der Braten | roast |
| die Soße (-n) | sauce |
| die Fleischsoße | gravy |
| der/das Curry | curry |
| die Wurst (¨e) | sausage |
| das Würstchen (-) | small sausage, chipolata |
| die Bockwurst (¨e) | bockwurst |
| die Bratwurst (¨e) | (fried) sausage |
| die Currywurst (¨e) | curried sausage |
| die Leberwurst (¨e) | liver sausage |
| die Frankfurter (¨e) | frankfurter |
| deutsches Beefsteak | hamburger, beefburger |
| der Hamburger (-) | hamburger |
| das Schnitzel (-) | veal/pork cutlet |
| die Frikadelle | rissole |
| paniert | coated with breadcrumbs |
| der Aufschnitt | sliced cold meat |
| die kalte Platte | cold meat |
| der Fisch (-e) | fish |
| die Forelle (-n) | trout |
| der Lachs (-e) | salmon |
| der Kabeljau (-e) | cod |

For restaurant food & snacks see Eating out, pages 94–5.

## j Die Kuchen — Cakes

|  |  |
|---|---|
| der Kuchen (-) | cake |
| der Apfelstrudel | apple strudel |
| der Apfelkuchen (-) | apple cake |
| der Keks (-e) | biscuit |
| das Plätzchen (-) | biscuit (*home-made*) |
| die Torte (-n) | gâteau, flan |
| der Pudding (-s) | flavoured custard dessert |
| die Sahne | cream |
| die Schlagsahne | whipped cream |
| die Creme | cream |
| die Vanille | vanilla |
| der Eisbecher | ice-cream sundae |
| die Süßigkeit (-en) / der/das Bonbon (-s) | sweet |
| der Beutel Bonbons | bag of sweets |
| die Rolle (-n) | tube |
| die Schokolade | chocolate (*general*) |
| die Praline (-n) | chocolate (*one sweet*) |
| die Schachtel Pralinen | box of chocolates |
| das Eis | ice-cream |
| die Tafel (-n) | bar, slab (*of chocolate*) |
| der Riegel (-) | bar |
| der Kaugummi | chewing gum |

|  |  |
|---|---|
| zunehmen (er nimmt zu) (s; sep) | to put on weight |
| abnehmen (er nimmt ab) (s; sep) | to lose weight |

## Jetzt bist du dran! 14

*Was gibt es hier zum essen?* — What is there to eat?

1. d _ _ B _ _ _ _ _ _
2. d _ _ K _ _ _ _ _
3. d _ _ F _ _ _ _ _
4. d _ _ oder H _ _ _ _ _ _ _ _
5. d _ _ A _ _ _ _ _ _
6. d _ _ B _ _ _

| | | |
|---|---|---|
| 7 | | d__ K___ |
| 8 | | d__ S_____ |
| 9 | | d__ B____ |
| 10 | | d__ P_____ f_____ |
| 11 | | d__ M____ oder K_____ |
| 12 | | zwei K_____ |

## k Getränke — Drinks

| | |
|---|---|
| trinken (er trinkt) (s) | to drink |
| das Getränk (-e) | drink |
| der Drink (-s) | drink (*alcoholic*) |
| die Erfrischung (-en) | refreshment |
| das Wasser | water |
| das Mineralwasser / der Sprudel | mineral water |
| die Milch | milk |
| der Saft | juice |
| der Fruchtsaft | fruit juice |
| der Apfelsaft | apple juice |
| der Orangensaft | orange juice |
| der Traubensaft | grape juice |
| der Tomatensaft | tomato juice |
| der Zitronensaft | lemon juice |
| die Limonade/die Limo | fizzy drink |
| die Zitronenlimonade | lemonade |
| die Cola | coke |
| der Eiswürfel (-) | ice cube |
| der Kakao | cocoa |
| der Tee | tea |
| der Teebeutel (-) | tea-bag |
| der Kaffee | coffee |
| der Alkohol | alcohol |
| alkoholfrei | non-alcoholic |
| alkoholisch | alcoholic |
| das Bier | beer |

| das Pilsner/das Pils (-) | Pilsner lager |
| ein Helles (*n*) | lager (*approx*) |
| ein Dunkles (*n*) | brown ale (*approx*) |
| der Wein | wine |
| der Weißwein | white wine |
| der Rotwein | red wine |
| der Sekt | German champagne |
| der Schnaps | spirits |

| einschenken (*sep*) | to pour out |
| das Glas (-̈er) | glass |
| zwei Glas Wein | two glasses of wine |
| die Maß (*S Germany only*) | litre (*of beer*) |

## Jetzt bist du dran! 15

| *Alphabet des Essens* | *Alphabet of food* |
|---|---|
| A  Geschnittene Wurst usw. | der A _ _ _ _ _ _ _ _ |
| B  Ganz schlecht für die Zähne. | der B _ _ _ _ _ |
| C  Im indischen Restaurant. | der C _ _ _ _ |
| D  Du brauchst einen Öffner dafür. | die D _ _ _ |
| E  Ein kleines, grünes, rundes Gemüse. | die E _ _ _ _ |
| F  Ein leckerer Fisch. | die F _ _ _ _ _ |
| G  Ein Vogel, den Deutsche gern essen. | die G _ _ _ |
| H  Eier für das Picknick. | h _ _ _ _ _ _ _ _ _ _ |
| I  Keine große Mahlzeit. | der I _ _ _ _ |
| J  Milchprodukt. | der J _ _ _ _ _ _ |
| K  Schmeckt, aber riecht stark! | der K _ _ _ _ _ _ _ _ |
| L  Eine grüne Frucht. | die L _ _ _ _ _ |
| M  Karotte. | die M _ _ _ _ |
| N  Frucht eines Baumes mit harter Schale. | die N _ _ |
| O  Man macht es mit Eiern. | das O _ _ _ _ _ _ |
| P  Sie wachsen auf der Wiese; manche sind giftig! | P _ _ _ _ |
| Q  Noch ein Milchprodukt! | der Q _ _ _ _ |
| R  Eine Art, Eier zu essen. | das R _ _ _ _ _ _ |
| S  Gelb und scharf; paßt gut zur Wurst. | der S _ _ _ |
| T  Ist es ein Obst oder ein Gemüse? | die T _ _ _ _ _ |
| U  z.B. zu viel Fett, oder zu wenig Gemüse. | u _ _ _ _ _ _ _ |
| V  „Normale" Milch. | die V _ _ _ _ _ _ _ _ |
| W  Typisches Fleischprodukt Deutschlands. | die W _ _ _ _ |
| Z  Gemüse. | die Z _ _ _ _ _ _ |

**Jetzt bist du dran! 16**

*Füll die Lücken aus! Unter den Sätzen sind mögliche Antworten, aber mehr als du brauchst!*

*Fill in the gaps. Below the sentences are possible answers (but more than you actually need).*

1 Die Scheiben Brot sind viel zu ____. Sandra will sie nicht!
2 Dieser Curry ist viel zu ____ für Holger.
3 Der Kaffee ist ja jetzt ____! Er ____ mir nicht mehr.
4 Einen ganzen ____ Schokolade essen? Lecker, aber ich ____ es nicht!
5 Du trinkst deinen Tee mit fünf ____ ____? Das ist viel zu ____ für mich.
6 „Magst du Rotkohl?" „Keine ____; ich habe ihn nie ____."
7 Die Milch ____ ich nicht trinken; sie ist zwei Tage ____ und schon ____.
8 Mir ____ ____ Gulasch nicht; er ist sehr ____.

---

Ahnung   alt   darf   dieser   dick   fett   gefällt
gefroren   Geschmack   kalt   kann   Löffeln   probiert
Riegel   sauer   scharf   schmeckt   sollte   süß
unappetitlich   will   Zucker

---

## 6 Gesundheit      Health

### a Die Körperteile      Parts of the body

| | |
|---|---|
| der Körper (-) | body |
| der Kopf (¨e) | head |
| das Haar (-e) | hair |
| das Ohr (-en) | ear |
| das Gesicht (-er) | face |
| die Stirn | forehead |
| die Augenbraue (-n) | eyebrow |
| die Wimpern (*pl*) | eyelashes |
| das Auge (-n) | eye |
| die Nase (-n) | nose |
| die Wange (-n) | cheek |
| die Lippe (-n) | lip |
| der Mund (¨er) | mouth |
| das Zahnfleisch | gum |

| | |
|---|---|
| der Zahn (¨e) | tooth |
| die Zunge (-n) | tongue |
| das Kinn (-e) | chin |
| | |
| der Hals (¨e) | neck, throat |
| die Schulter (-n) | shoulder |
| der Arm (-e) | arm |
| der Ellenbogen (-) | elbow |
| das Handgelenk (-e) | wrist |
| die Hand (¨e) | hand |
| der Finger (-) | finger |
| der Daumen (-) | thumb |
| der Fingernagel (¨) | nail |
| | |
| der Rücken (-) | back |
| die Brust (¨e) | breast, chest |
| der Magen (-) | stomach |
| der Bauch (¨e) | stomach, tummy |
| die Taille (-n) | waist |
| das Bein (-e) | leg |
| der Schenkel (-) | thigh |
| das Knie (-) | knee |
| der Fuß (Füße) | foot |
| der Knöchel (-) | ankle |
| die Zehe (-n) | toe |
| | |
| der Muskel (-n) | muscle |
| das Herz (-en) | heart |
| die Lunge (-n) | lung |
| der Knochen (-) | bone |
| die Haut | skin |
| das Blut | blood |
| der Schweiß | sweat |
| schwitzen | to sweat |
| gähnen | to yawn |
| atmen | to breathe |
| der Schluckauf | hiccups |
| aua! | ow! |
| sich bewegen (*insep*) | to move |

 See also under What people look like, pages 58–60.

**Jetzt bist du dran! 17**

*Finde das richtige Wort für die Köperteile!*

Find the names for the parts of the body indicated.

## b Schmerzen — Aches and pains

| | |
|---|---|
| ich habe Hunger | I am hungry |
| hungrig | hungry |
| ich habe Durst | I am thirsty |
| durstig | thirsty |
| mir ist heiß/kalt | I am hot/cold |
| mir ist schwind(e)lig | I feel dizzy |
| ohnmächtig werden* (s) | to faint |
| wieder zu sich (*Dat*) kommen* | to come round |
| ich fühle mich komisch | I feel funny/odd |
| mir ist übel/schlecht | I feel sick |
| kotzen (*colloquial*) | to throw up |
| sich übergeben (er übergibt sich) (s; *insep*) | to vomit |
| ich fühle mich nicht wohl | I don't feel too well |
| krank | ill, sick |
| leiden (er leidet) (s) | to suffer |

| | |
|---|---|
| ich habe Schmerzen | I have a pain |
| der Schmerz (-en) | pain |
| weh tun (+*Dat*) (es tut weh) (*s*) | to hurt |
| Bauchschmerzen (*pl*) }<br>das Bauchweh } | stomach ache |
| mir tun die Füße weh | my feet hurt |
| einen Krampf haben | to have cramp |
| eine Magenverstimmung | upset stomach |
| der Durchfall | diarrhoea |
| verstopft | constipated |
| die Verstopfung | constipation |
| | |
| Halsschmerzen (*pl*) | sore throat |
| Kopfschmerzen (*pl*) | headache |
| Zahnschmerzen (*pl*) | toothache |
| | |
| der Sonnenbrand | sunburn |
| der Sonnenstich | sunstroke |
| der Insektenstich (-e) | insect bite |
| jucken | to itch |
| es juckt mich am Rücken }<br>der Rücken juckt mich } | my back itches |
| kratzen | to scratch |
| | |
| stürzen* | to fall over |
| verunglücken* (*insep*) | to have an accident |
| verwunden (*insep*) | to wound |
| die Wunde (-n) | wound |
| verletzen (verletzt) | to injure (injured) |
| die Verletzung (-en) | injury |
| brechen (er bricht) (*s*) | to break |
| ich habe mir den Arm gebrochen | I have broken my arm |
| einen Arm in Gips haben | to have an arm in plaster |
| ich habe mir den Fuß vertreten (*s*) | I have twisted my ankle |
| geschwollen | swollen |
| | |
| das Pflaster/Heftpflaster (-) | sticking-plaster |
| das Hansapflast ® | Elastoplast ® |
| ein Pflaster aufkleben (*sep*) | to put on a plaster |
| weinen | to cry, weep |
| die Erste Hilfe | first aid |
| Erste Hilfe leisten | to give first aid |
| retten | to save |

| | |
|---|---|
| **der Atem** | breath |
| **atemlos** | breathless |
| **fit** | fit |
| **gesund** | healthy |
| **es geht ihm wieder besser** | he is better |
| **betrunken** | drunk |
| **der Kater** | hangover |

## Jetzt bist du dran! 18

*Stell dir die folgenden Situationen vor. Wo tut es dir weh? Was sagst du zu einem Freund?*

*Imagine the following situations. Where does it hurt? What do you tell a friend?*

**Beispiel:** *Ich wollte den Topf aufnehmen, aber er war zu heiß.*
= *Der Finger tut mir weh./Die Finger tun mir weh.*

1 *Ich bin vom Fahrrad gestürzt.*
2 *Zerbrochene Flaschen waren am Strand, wo ich gelaufen bin.*
3 *Das kleine Kind hat mir Sand ins Gesicht geworfen.*
4 *Ich habe den Eimer Wasser fallenlassen.*
5 *Ich wollte den Sack aufheben, aber er war zu schwer für mich.*
6 *Wir spielten Hockey, und ich bin mit dem Schläger getroffen worden.*
7 *Jemand hat mir mit der Faust ins Gesicht geschlagen.*
8 *Die Lampe hing sehr tief, und ich bin dagegen gelaufen.*
9 *Ich putze mir sehr selten die Zähne.*
10 *Ich habe beim Fußballspiel zu viel geschrien.*

## c Krankheiten — Illnesses

| | |
|---|---|
| **die Krankheit (-en)** | illness |
| **krank** | ill |
| **was fehlt dir/Ihnen?** ⎫ | |
| **was ist los?** ⎭ | what's wrong? |
| **sich (nicht) wohl fühlen** | (not) to feel well |
| **sich unwohl fühlen** | to feel unwell |
| **ich fühle mich etwas unwohl** | I feel a bit unwell |
| **die Allergie (-n) (gegen etwas)** | allergy (to something) |
| **allergisch (gegen...)** | allergic (to...) |
| **ich bin erkältet** ⎫ | |
| **ich habe eine Erkältung** ⎬ | I have a cold |
| **ich habe Schnupfen** ⎭ | |

| | |
|---|---|
| husten | to cough |
| der Husten | cough |
| niesen | to sneeze |
| die Grippe haben | to have the flu |
| Fieber haben | to have a temperature |
| 38 Grad Fieber haben | to have a (high) temperature of 38° C |
| schwitzen | to sweat |
| die Gänsehaut | goosepimples |
| der Heuschnupfen | hay fever |
| der Ausschlag (¨e) | rash |
| der Pickel | spot, pimple |
| die Masern (*pl*) | measles |
| der/die Mumps | mumps |
| die Windpocken (*pl*) | chicken-pox |
| AIDS | AIDS |
| bluten | to bleed |
| ich habe Nasenbluten | I have a nose bleed |
| sich übergeben (er übergibt sich) (*s; insep*) | to vomit |
| ich bin seekrank | I feel sea-sick |
| die Seekrankheit | sea-sickness |
| (körper)behindert | (physically) disabled |
| blind | blind |
| stumm | dumb |
| taub | deaf |

 See also Death, page 52.

## d Beim Arzt — At the doctor's

| | |
|---|---|
| der Arzt (¨e) | doctor (*male or general word*) |
| die Ärztin (-nen) | doctor (*f*) |
| die Sprechstunde (-n) | surgery hours |
| der Termin (-e) | appointment |
| einen Termin vereinbaren (*insep*) | to make an appointment |
| betreuen (*insep*) | to look after |
| behandeln (*insep*) | to treat |
| untersuchen (*insep*) | to examine |
| das Thermometer (-) | thermometer |
| messen (er mißt) (*s*) | to measure |

| | |
|---|---|
| er hat meine Temperatur gemessen | he took my temperature |
| die Blutprobe | blood-test |
| der Blutdruck | blood pressure |
| verbinden (er verbindet) (*s; insep*) | to bandage up |
| der Verband (-"e) | bandage |
| die Spritze (-n) | injection/syringe |
| raten (er rät) (+*Dat*) (*s*) | to advise |
| sich hinlegen (*sep*) | to lie down |
| sich ausruhen (*sep*) | to rest, relax |
| sich erholen (*insep*) | to recover |
| eine Kur machen | to undergo a cure/health treatment |
| der Kurort (-e) | health resort, spa |
| sich bewegen (*insep*) | to get exercise, move |
| zunehmen (er nimmt zu) (*s; sep*) | to put on weight |
| abnehmen (er nimmt ab) (*s; sep*) | to lose weight |
| eine Schlankheitskur/Diät machen | to go on a diet |
| genesen* (er genest) (*s; insep*) | to recover, recuperate |
| zwei Tage (lang) | for two days |
| im Bett bleiben* (er bleibt) (*s*) | to stay in bed |
| gesund | healthy |
| (nicht) schlimm | (not) serious |
| keine Sorge! | don't worry! |
| gute Besserung! | get well soon |
| das Rezept (-e) | prescription |
| die Krankenkasse (-n) | medical insurance scheme |
| der Krankenschein (-e) | certificate of medical insurance |
| AOK (Allgemeine Ortskrankenkasse) | German medical insurance company |
| der E111-Schein (-e) | E111 (*medical cover for EU members travelling within EU*) |
| schwanger | pregnant |
| die Schwangerschaft (-en) | pregnancy |

## e In der Apotheke

## At the chemist's

| | |
|---|---|
| der Apotheker (-) <br> die Apothekerin (-nen) } | pharmacist (*m/f*) |
| das Rezept (-e) | prescription |
| dreimal pro Tag | three times a day |
| vor/nach dem Essen | before/after meals |
| das Medikament (-e) | medicine |

| | |
|---|---|
| ein Löffel Medizin | one spoonful of medicine |
| zweimal pro Tag einnnehmen (er nimmt … ein) *(s)* | to take/be taken twice a day *(dosage instructions)* |
| die Pille (-n) | pill |
| eine Tablette nehmen (er nimmt) *(s)* | to take a tablet |
| der Tropfen (-) | drop |
| die Kopfschmerztablette (-n) | painkiller |
| das Aspirin ® | aspirin ® |
| der Hustenbonbon (-s) | cough sweet |
| die Salbe | ointment |
| die Watte | cotton wool |
| wischen | to wipe |
| schlucken | to swallow |
| das Pflaster (-) | sticking plaster |
| die Dosierung | dosage |

## f Im Krankenhaus — In hospital

| | |
|---|---|
| das Krankenhaus (¨-er) | hospital |
| die Klinik (-en) | university hospital, clinic |
| der Chirurg (-en, -en) ⎫ die Chirurgin (-nen) ⎭ | surgeon *(m/f)* |
| die Oberschwester (-n) | sister |
| der Krankenpfleger (-) ⎫ die Krankenschwester (-n) ⎭ | nurse *(m/f)* |
| pflegen | to nurse, to look after |
| sich röntgen lassen | to be X-rayed |
| operiert werden* *(s)* | to have an operation |
| operieren | to operate |
| der Patient (-en, -en) ⎫ die Patientin (-nen) ⎭ | patient *(m/f)* |
| (nicht) in Lebensgefahr | (not) in a critical condition |
| das Krankenzimmer (-) | ward *(small)* |
| die Station | ward |
| der Krankenwagen (-) | ambulance |

## g Die Sucht — Addiction

| | |
|---|---|
| rauchen | to smoke |
| der Raucher (-)/die Raucherin | smoker *(m/f)* |
| der Tabak | tobacco |
| die Zigarette (-n) | cigarette |
| die Zigarre (-n) | cigar |

| | |
|---|---|
| die Pfeife (-n) | pipe |
| hast du Feuer? | do you have a light? |
| das Feuerzeug | lighter |
| das Streichholz (¨er) | match |
| der Aschenbecher (-) | ashtray |
| angeben (er gibt an) (*s; sep*) | to show off |
| der Erwartungsdruck | peer pressure |
| husten | to cough |
| schädlich | harmful |
| der Lungenkrebs | lung cancer |
| die Herzkrankheit | heart disease |

| | |
|---|---|
| der Alkohol | alcohol |
| der Alkoholismus | alcoholism |
| betrunken | |
| blau (*colloquial*) } | drunk |
| die Betrunkenheit | drunkenness |
| der Trinker (-)/die Trinkerin (-nen) | |
| der Säufer (-)/die Säuferin (-nen) } | drunkard |

| | |
|---|---|
| die Droge (-n) | drug |
| das Rauschgift | drug(s) |
| harte Drogen (*pl*) | hard drugs |
| weiche Drogen (*pl*) | soft drugs |
| die Drogenszene | the drugs scene |
| die Spritze (-n) | syringe |
| der Drogensüchtige (*adj. noun*) | drug addict |
| der Dealer | drug dealer |
| (drogen)abhängig werden* (*s*) | to get hooked |
| die Sucht | dependency, addiction |
| die Dauerwirkung (-en) | long-term effect |
| die Überdosis | overdose |
| verzichten auf (+*Acc*) | to do without |

## h Der Tod — Death

| | |
|---|---|
| sterben* (er stirbt) (*s*) | to die |
| tot | dead |
| die Leiche (-n) | corpse |
| beerdigen (*insep*) | to bury |
| die Beerdigung (-en) | burial |
| das Begräbnis | funeral |
| der Friedhof (¨e) | cemetery |

# B: Personal and social life

## 1 Verwandte und Bekannte
## Family and friends

### a Darf ich mich vorstellen?
### May I introduce myself?

| | |
|---|---|
| heißen (er heißt) (s) | to be called |
| nennen (er nennt) (irreg w) | to call |
| der Name (-ns, -n) | name |
| der Vorname (-ns, -n) | Christian name |
| der Familienname (-ns, -n) | surname |
| der Mädchenname (-ns, -n) | maiden name |
| wie heißt du? | what is your name? |
| wie heißt er mit Vornamen? | what is his Christian name? |
| soll ich ihn buchstabieren? | shall I spell it? |
| er schreibt sich... | it is spelt... |
| unterschreiben (er unterschreibt) (s; insep) | to sign one's name |
| die Unterschrift (-en) | signature |
| | |
| wohnen (in...+place) | to live (in...) |
| leben | to live, to be alive |
| wo kommst du her? | where do you come from? |
| die Adresse (-n) } die Anschrift (-en) } | address |
| allein | alone |
| der Wohnort | place of residence |
| der Wohnsitz (-e) | domicile |
| die Heimatstadt (¨e) | home town |
| die Postleitzahl | post code |
| die Hausnummer (-n) | house number |
| die Straße (-n) | street, road |
| der Weg (-e) | way, path |
| die Allee (-n) | avenue |
| der Platz (¨e) | square |
| das Telefon (-e) | telephone |
| wir haben (kein) Telefon | we are (not) on the phone |
| die Vorwahl (-en) | area dialling code |
| die Durchwahl (-en) | direct number (eg in an office) |

| | |
|---|---|
| **alt** | old |
| **jung** | young |
| **das Alter** | age |
| **wie alt bist du?** | how old are you? |
| **ich bin vierzehn (Jahre alt)** | I am fourteen (years old) |
| **ich werde fünfzehn** | I am nearly fifteen |
| **das Jahr (-e)** | year |
| **der Monat (-e)** | month |
| **ich bin 1985 in Ely geboren** | I was born in 1985 in Ely |
| **die Geburt (-en)** | birth |
| **das Geburtsdatum** | date of birth |
| **der Geburtsort** | place of birth |
| **die Heimat** | home town/native country |
| **stammen aus (+*Dat*)** | to come from |
| | |
| **der/die Jugendliche (*adj. noun*)** | young person, teenager |
| **der Teenager (-)** | teenager |
| **der/die Erwachsene (*adj. noun*)** | adult |
| | |
| **das Geschlecht (-er)** | sex |
| **männlich** | male |
| **weiblich** | female |
| | |
| **die Religion** | religion |
| **christlich** | Christian |
| **evangelisch** } **protestantisch** | Protestant |
| **katholisch** | Roman Catholic |
| **jüdisch/Jude** | Jewish |
| **Mohammedaner/Moslem** | Moslem |
| **Hindu** | Hindu |
| **Sikh** | Sikh |
| **keine** | none |
| | |
| **die Staatsangehörigkeit** | nationality |
| **Deutscher/Deutsche (*adj. noun*)** | German (of *person m/f*) |
| **Engländer/Engländerin** | English (of *person m/f*) |
| **Brite/Britin** | British (of *person m/f*) |
| **der Ausweis (-e)** | identity card |
| **sich ausweisen (er weist sich aus) (*s; sep*)** | to produce identification |

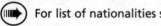 For list of nationalities see pages 173–4.

# Jetzt bist du dran! 19

Füll das Formular in
Großbuchstaben aus!

Fill in the form using block
capitals

---

BITTE IN GROSSBUCHSTABEN AUSFÜLLEN!

Name:

.......................................................................................

Vornamen: ..........................................................................

Wohnort: .............................................................................

.......................................................................................

Telefon: ..............................................................................

Religion: .............................................................................

Geburtsdatum: ....................................................................

Geburtsort: ........................................................................

Staatsangehörigkeit: ...........................................................

Ausweisnummer: ...................................

Paßnummer: ...........................................

Ausgestellt in: .......................................

Beruf: ....................................................

Größe: ..................................................

Augen: ................................................................................

Datum: ................................................................................

Unterschrift: ........................................................................

Lichtbild

---

## b Familie — Family

| | |
|---|---|
| der Mensch (-en, -en) | person/human being |
| die Person (-en) | person |
| der Mann (¨er) | man/husband |
| der Herr (-n, -en) | gentleman |
| die Frau (-en) | woman/wife |
| die Dame (-n) | lady |
| das Kind (-er) | child |
| das Baby (-s) | baby |
| der Junge (-n, -n) | boy |
| das Mädchen (-) | girl |
| die Familie (-n) | family |
| Herr... | Mr... |
| Frau... | Mrs.../Ms... |
| Fräulein... | Miss... |

| | |
|---|---|
| der/die Verwandte (adj. noun) | relation, relative (m/f) |
| die Eltern (pl only) | parents |
| der Vater (¨) | father |
| der Vati (-s) | dad |
| die Mutter (¨) | mother |
| die Mutti (-s) | mum |
| die Geschwister (pl) | brothers and sisters, siblings |
| der Bruder (¨) | brother |
| die Schwester (-n) | sister |
| der Zwilling (-e) | twin |
| der Zwillingsbruder (¨) | twin brother |
| die Zwillingsschwester (-n) | twin sister |
| der Sohn (¨e) | son |
| die Tochter (¨) | daughter |
| Stief- (Stiefvater usw) | step- (stepfather etc) |
| Halb- (Halbbruder usw) | half- (half brother etc) |
| der Onkel (-) | uncle |
| die Tante (-n) | aunt |
| der Neffe (-n, -n) | nephew |
| die Nichte (-n) | niece |
| die (Ur)großeltern (pl) | (great) grand-parents |
| der Großvater (-) | grandfather |
| der Opa (-s) | grandad |
| die Großmutter (¨) | grandmother |
| die Oma (-s) | granny |
| der Enkel (-) | grandson |
| die Enkelin (-nen) | granddaughter |

| | |
|---|---|
| der Cousin (-s) }<br>der Vetter (-) } | boy cousin |
| die Kusine (-n) }<br>die Cousine (-n) } | girl cousin |
| der Schwager (⁻:) | brother-in-law |
| die Schwägerin (-nen) | sister-in-law |
| d.. Schwieger- | ...-in-law |
| die Schwiegereltern | parents-in-law |
| der Pate (-n, -n)/Patenonkel (-) | godfather |
| die Patin (-nen)/Patentante (-n) | godmother |

| | |
|---|---|
| der Mann (Ehemann) (⁻er) | husband |
| die Frau (Ehefrau) (-en) | wife |
| das Ehepaar (-e) | married couple |
| der Partner (-) | partner (male) |
| die Partnerin (-nen) | partner (female) |
| der/die Verlobte (adj. noun) | fiancé(e) |
| heiraten | to marry |
| mein Bruder ist schon seit zwei Jahren verheiratet | my brother has been married for two years |
| meine Schwester heiratet im Juli | my sister is getting married in July |

| | |
|---|---|
| der Familienstand (⁻e) | marital status |
| (un)verheiratet | (un)married |
| ledig | single |
| getrennt | separated |
| geschieden | divorced |
| der Witwer (-) | widower |
| die Witwe (-n) | widow |

| | |
|---|---|
| alt | old |
| älter/jünger als | older/younger than |
| ältest- | eldest |
| jung | young |
| jüngst- | youngest |
| ich bin die Älteste | I'm the eldest |
| ich bin Einzelkind | I'm an only child |
| ich bin adoptiert | I'm adopted |
| wir sind vier | there are four of us |

| | |
|---|---|
| die Kindheit | childhood |
| die Jugend | youth |
| Jugendliche (pl) (adj. noun) | young people |
| volljährig/mündig | major (over 18) |

| | |
|---|---|
| **minderjährig** | minor (under 18) |
| **der/die Erwachsene** (*adj. noun*) | adult |
| **in den mittleren Jahren** | middle-aged |
| **der Rentner (-)** ⎫<br>**die Rentnerin (-nen)** ⎭ | old age pensioner (*m/f*) |
| **tot** | dead |
| **verstorben** | deceased |
| **meine Urgroßeltern sind alle verstorben** | my great-grandparents are all dead |

## Jetzt bist du dran! 20

*Welche Verwandten beschreibt man? Findest du heraus, welches Wort in die Lücke gehört?*

*Which relations are being described? Can you find the missing word?*

1 Der Sohn meines Bruders ist mein _ _ _ _ _.
2 Die Mutter von Jürgens Vati ist seine _ _ _ _ _ _ _ _ _ _.
3 Die Tochter von Onkel Kurts Tochter ist seine _ _ _ _ _ _ _ _.
4 Der Sohn von Muttis Schwester ist unser _ _ _ _ _ _ _ oder unser _ _ _ _ _ _.
5 Opa und Oma sind unsere _ _ _ _ _ _ _ _ _ _.
6 Wolfgangs Muttis neuer Mann ist sein _ _ _ _ _ _ _ _ _ _.
7 Die Frau meines Bruders ist meine _ _ _ _ _ _ _ _ _ _.
8 Der Vater und die Mutter von Ingrids Mann sind ihre _ _ _ _ _ _ _ _ _ _ _ _ _ _.
9 Ulrichs Bruder, der am selben Tag geboren ist wie er, ist sein _ _ _ _ _ _ _ _ _ _ _ _ _ _ _.
10 Sophie hat denselben Vater wie Andreas aber eine andere Mutter; sie ist also seine _ _ _ _ _ _ _ _ _ _ _ _ _.

## c Wie die Leute aussehen

## What people look like

| | |
|---|---|
| **aussehen (er sieht ... aus)**<br>**(s; sep)** | to look (+*adj.*) |
| **das Aussehen** | appearance |
| **erkennen (er erkennt)**<br>**(irreg w; insep)** | to recognise |
| **was für ein ...?** | what sort of...? |
| **ähnlich (+Dat)** | similar |
| **er ist seinem Bruder sehr ähnlich** | he is very like his brother |

| | |
|---|---|
| er ist sehr anders als sein Bruder | he is very different from his brother |
| sie sind sehr verschieden | they are very different |

| | |
|---|---|
| groß | tall |
| klein | short |
| mittelgroß | of average height |
| enorm | enormous |
| dick | fat |
| schlank | slim |
| mager | thin |
| athletisch | athletic |
| stämmig | stocky |
| muskulös | muscular |
| stark | strong |
| schwach | weak |
| schön | beautiful, handsome |
| hübsch | pretty |
| gutaussehend | good-looking |
| häßlich | ugly |
| blaß | pale |

| | |
|---|---|
| etwas klein | |
| ein wenig klein | slightly short |
| ein bißchen klein | |
| ziemlich klein | fairly short |
| gar nicht klein | not at all short |
| ganz klein | really short |
| (nicht) besonders klein | (not) especially short |

| | |
|---|---|
| der Körper (-) | body |
| der Kopf (¨e) | head |
| die Glatze (-n) | bald patch |
| das Gesicht (-er) | face |
| dünn | thin |
| rund | round |
| flach | flat |
| blaß | pale |
| die Sommersprossen (pl) | freckles |
| der Pickel (-) | spot, pimple |

| | |
|---|---|
| das Auge (-n) | eye |
| grün | green |
| blau | blue |

| | |
|---|---|
| grau | grey |
| braun | brown |

| | |
|---|---|
| der Mund (¨er) | mouth |
| schmal | narrow |
| breit | wide |
| die Lippe (-n) | lip |
| der Zahn (¨e) | tooth |
| die Zunge (-n) | tongue |

| | |
|---|---|
| das Haar (-e) | hair |
| kurz | short |
| lang | long |
| mittellang | of medium length |
| wellig | wavy |
| lockig | curly |
| schwarz | black |
| blond | blond |
| dunkelblond | dark blond, light brown |
| hell | fair |
| grau | grey |
| weiß | white |
| blondgefärbt | dyed blond |
| mit blonden Strähnen | with blond streaks |

| | |
|---|---|
| der Bart (¨e) | beard |
| der Backenbart (¨e) | sideboards |
| der Schnurrbart (¨e) | moustache |
| die Nase (-n) | nose |
| spitz | pointed |
| breit | broad |
| das Ohr (-en) | ear |

## Jetzt bist du dran! 21

*Denk an drei Leute in deiner Familie und an drei andere Freunde! Beschreib sie!*

*Think of three members of your family and three other friends. Make up sentences to describe them.*

Beispiel: *Mein Großvater hat graue Haare.*

➡️ Wer hat:
blaue Augen?
sehr wenig Haar?
dunkelbraunes Haar?
kurze Beine?
eine große Nase?
Pickel?
braune Augen?
dunkelblonde Haare?

breite Schultern?
einen Bart?
weißes Haar?
einen dicken Bauch?
ein ovales Gesicht?
mittellanges Haar?
eine Spitznase?
Sommersprossen?
einen großen Mund?

# Jetzt bist du dran! 22

Beschreib dich selbst, dann die
Mitglieder deiner Familie.
Einige Sätze sind schon voll
ausgeschrieben aber mach neue
Sätze, wenn diese nicht stimmen.

Describe yourself and the
members of your family.
Some sentences are already
done for you.

| | Wie groß? | Augen | Haare | Gesicht | Körperbau | Brille? |
|---|---|---|---|---|---|---|
| Ich | | | | | Ich bin schlank. | |
| Mutti | Sie ist ziemlich klein. | | | | | |
| Vati | Er ist 1,80 Meter groß. | | | | Er wiegt 70 Kilogramm. | |
| Oma | | | Sie hat graue Haare. | | | Sie trägt ziemlich oft eine Brille. |
| Opa | | Er hat grüne Augen. | | | | |
| Bruder | | | | | Er ist stämmig. | |
| Schwester | | | | Sie hat ein rundes Gesicht. | | Sie trägt keine Brille. |
| Freund | | | | | Er ist athletisch. | |
| Freundin | | | Sie hat lange, wellige Haare. | | | |

## d Charakter und Gefühle    Character and feelings

| | |
|---|---|
| ehrlich | honest |
| ernst | serious |
| fleißig | hard-working |
| geduldig | patient |
| ruhig | calm |
| sicher | certain, sure |

| | |
|---|---|
| glücklich | happy |
| zum Glück } glücklicherweise | fortunately |
| gut gelaunt | in a good mood |
| sich freuen | to be glad |
| es freut mich | I am glad |
| ich bin froh, daß... | I am glad that... |
| hoffen | to hope |
| hoffentlich | it is to be hoped that |
| lebhaft | lively |
| lustig | funny, amusing |
| er ist lustig | he is fun/funny |
| es macht Spaß, mit ihm zusammen zu sein | he is fun to be with |
| lachen | to laugh |
| lächeln | to smile |
| nett } sympathisch | nice |
| süß | sweet |
| freundlich | friendly |
| höflich | polite |
| intelligent | intelligent |
| klug | clever |
| neugierig | inquisitive |
| offen | frank, open |
| das ist typisch für ihn! | that's typical of him! |
| (un)interessant | (un)interesting |
| ich habe recht | I am right |
| raten (+Dat) (er rät) (s) | to advise |

| | |
|---|---|
| blöd | silly |
| doof (colloquial) | stupid |
| dumm | stupid |
| unintelligent | unintelligent |

| | |
|---|---|
| **schlecht** | bad (*poor quality*) |
| **schlimm** | wicked, naughty |
| **zornig** | angry |
| **böse** | angry, nasty, naughty |
| **ärgern** | to annoy |
| **sich ärgern (über…) (+*Acc*)** | to get/be annoyed (about…) |
| **streiten (er streitet) (*s*)** | to quarrel |
| **der Krach** | quarrel |
| **schlecht gelaunt** | in a bad mood |
| **traurig** | sad, unhappy |
| **unglücklich** | unhappy |

| | |
|---|---|
| **enttäuscht (von…) (+*Dat*)** | disappointed (with…) |
| **die Enttäuschung (-en)** | disappointment |
| **es tut mir leid** | I am sorry |
| **ich schäme mich** | I am ashamed |
| **es ist zu bedauern** | it is regrettable |
| **das ist (zu) schade** | it's a (real) shame |
| **leider** | unfortunately |
| **das kann nicht sein** | that cannot be true |
| **ich habe unrecht** | I am wrong |

| | |
|---|---|
| **nervös** | nervous |
| **schüchtern** | shy |
| **unfreundlich** } | |
| **unsympathisch** } | unfriendly |
| **langweilig** | boring |
| **ich finde ihn langweilig** | I think he's boring |
| **frech** | cheeky |
| **egoistisch** | selfish |
| **faul** | lazy |
| **ungeduldig** | impatient |
| **unhöflich** | rude |
| **unehrlich** | dishonest |

## Jetzt bist du dran! 23

Man kann hier Wörter über das Aussehen, den Körper und den Charakter finden. Man liest nach oben oder nach unten, vorwärts oder rückwärts. Es gibt etwa 20!

Find words about appearance, the body and character. They read up or down, forwards or backwards. There are about 20!

| | | | | | | | | | | |
|---|---|---|---|---|---|---|---|---|---|---|
| H | E | N | Ő | H | C | S | U | G | F | G | I |
| A | H | E | L | L | O | T | N | E | R | I | N |
| À | C | U | H | N | Z | A | H | N | E | T | T |
| R | S | G | C | N | E | R | Ő | I | U | S | E |
| E | I | I | S | Ú | G | K | F | E | N | U | R |
| P | T | E | B | D | N | O | L | B | D | L | E |
| R | S | R | Ú | E | U | P | I | A | L | A | S |
| O | I | E | H | E | Z | F | C | R | I | U | S |
| K | O | D | F | R | E | C | H | T | C | N | A |
| A | G | I | K | C | O | L | A | C | H | E | N |
| W | E | L | L | I | G | I | R | U | A | R | T |
| H | C | S | I | H | T | A | P | M | Y | S | A |

## e Andere Leute kennenlernen

## Meeting people

| | |
|---|---|
| **treffen (er trifft) (s)** | to meet |
| **begegnen\* (+Dat) (insep)** | to meet (*by accident*) |
| **durch Zufall** | by chance |
| **abholen (sep)** | to meet, fetch (*eg at station*) |
| **sich (Acc) vorstellen (sep)** | to introduce oneself |
| **begrüßen (insep)** | to greet, to welcome |
| **willkommen in Deutschland!** | welcome to Germany |
| **freut mich!** | pleased to meet you! |
| **wie geht es dir/Ihnen?** | how are you? |
| **lächeln** | to smile |
| **sich (Dat) die Hand geben (er gibt) (s)** | to shake hands |
| **umarmen (insep)** | to embrace, hug |
| **küssen** | to kiss |
| **der Kuß (Küsse)** | kiss |
| **kennenlernen (sep)** | to get to know |
| **bekannt machen (mit...)** | to introduce (to...) |
| **der Gast (-̈e)** | guest (*m/f*) |
| **der Gastgeber (-)** | host |
| **die Gastgeberin (-nen)** | hostess |

| | |
|---|---|
| gastfreundlich | hospitable |
| die Gastfreundschaft | hospitality |
| das Gastgeschenk (-e) | present brought by visitor |
| das Gästezimmer (-) | guest room |
| der Partner/Austauschpartner (-) | (exchange) partner (*m*) |
| die Partnerin/ Austauschpartnerin(-in) | (exchange) partner (*f*) |
| der Brieffreund (-e) | penfriend (*m*) |
| die Brieffreundin (-nen) | penfriend (*f*) |

## f Grüße — Greetings

| | |
|---|---|
| guten Morgen | good morning |
| guten Tag | hello |
| Servus (*S German/Austrian*) | hello/goodbye |
| tschüs | bye |
| auf Wiedersehen | goodbye |
| auf Wiederhören | goodbye (*on phone*) |
| guten Abend | good evening |
| gute Nacht | good night |
| schönes Wochenende | have a good weekend |
| bis später | see you later |
| bis bald | see you soon |
| bis morgen | see you tomorrow |

| | |
|---|---|
| alles Gute | all the best |
| viel Spaß | have fun |
| mach's gut | take care |

## f Beziehungen — Relationships

| | |
|---|---|
| der Freund (-e) | friend (*m*)/boyfriend |
| die Freundin (-nen) | friend (*f*)/girlfriend |

| | |
|---|---|
| ich habe ihn (nicht) gern <br> ich mag ihn (nicht) (gern) | I (don't) like him |
| ich kann ihn gut leiden | I like him |
| ich kann ihn nicht leiden | I cannot stand him |
| sich gut vertragen (er verträgt sich) (*s; insep*) | to get on well |
| ich habe (keine) Angst (vor ihm) | I am (not) afraid (of him) |
| lieben | to love |
| hassen | to hate |
| lieb | kind, nice |

| | |
|---|---|
| brav | kind, good |
| nett | nice |
| angenehm | pleasant |
| er ist gut zu mir | he is good to me |
| er ist ein guter Freund | he is a good friend to me |
| gut befreundet sein | to be good friends |
| (un)freundlich }<br>(un)sympathisch } | (un)friendly |
| (un)beliebt | (un)popular |
| trauen (+*Dat*) | to trust |
| ich traue ihm wenig | I don't trust him much |

### g Vergleiche anstellen

### Making comparisons

| | |
|---|---|
| er ist älter als ich | he is older than I am |
| er ist (genau)so alt wie ich | he is (exactly) as old as I am |
| genauso | just as |
| er ist nicht so alt wie ich | he is not as old as I am |
| er ist fast so alt wie ich | he is nearly as old as I am |
| wir sind gleich groß | we are as tall as each other |
| er ist der Ältere | he is the elder/older one |
| er ist der Älteste }<br>er ist am ältesten } | he is the eldest/oldest |
| er ist wie ich | he is like me |
| er ist anders als ich | he is different from me |
| ähnlich (+*Dat*) | similar to |

## 2 Zu Hause

## At home

### a Allgemeines

### General

| | |
|---|---|
| einziehen* in (+*Acc*) (s; sep) | to move in |
| umziehen* (s; sep) }<br>die Wohnung wechseln } | to move house |
| ausziehen* aus (+*Acc*) (er zieht<br>... aus) (*s; sep*) | to move out |

| | |
|---|---|
| das Gebäude (-) | building |
| das Haus (¨er) | house, block of flats |
| das Einfamilienhaus (¨er) | detached house |
| das Doppelhaus (¨er) | semi-detached house |
| das Reihenhaus (¨er) | terraced house |
| das Häuschen (-) | cottage, little house |
| der Bungalow (-s) | bungalow |

| | |
|---|---|
| die Wohnung (-en) | flat, dwelling in general |
| der Wohnblock (-s) | block of flats |
| das Hochhaus (¨er) | high-rise building |
| die Siedlung (-en) | estate |
| die Sozialwohnung (-en) | council flat/house |
| der Bauernhof (¨e) | farm |

| | |
|---|---|
| der Stock (Stockwerke) }<br>die Etage (-n) } | storey, floor |
| das Erdgeschoß | ground floor |
| im ersten/zweiten Stock | on the 1st/2nd floor |
| das Obergeschoß | upper/top floor |
| der Keller (-) | cellar |
| der Dachboden (¨) }<br>die Mansarde (-n) } | attic |
| der Speicher (-) | loft |
| das Dach (¨er) | roof |
| der Schornstein (-e) | chimney |

| | |
|---|---|
| bauen | to build |
| 1900 gebaut | built in 1900 |
| anbauen (*sep*) | to build an extension |
| der Anbau (-ten) | extension |
| alt | old |
| neu | new |
| modern | modern |
| altmodisch | old fashioned |
| modernisiert | modernised |
| nett | nice, charming |
| gemütlich | comfortable, cosy |
| praktisch | practical |

| | |
|---|---|
| (un)bequem | (un)comfortable/(in)convenient |
| (un)möbliert | (un)furnished |
| (un)interessant | (un)interesting |

| | |
|---|---|
| die Lage (-n) | situation, position |
| der/das Quadratmeter (-) | square metre |

| | |
|---|---|
| die Miete (-n) | rent |
| mieten | to rent (*from someone*) |
| vermieten (*insep*) | to rent out (*to someone*) |
| der Nachbar (-n, -n) | neighbour (*m*) |
| die Nachbarin (-nen) | neighbour (*f*) |

**der Hausmeister (-)**
**die Hausmeisterin (-nen)** } caretaker (*m/f*)

---

 **Jetzt bist du dran! 24**

*Unterstreich die Wörter, die dieses Haus beschreiben.*

*Underline the words that describe this house.*

1 Das Haus ist...
groß        altmodisch
ein Einfamilienhaus        klein
modern        ein Doppelhaus

2 Es hat...
eine Etage        einen Dachboden

zwei Stockwerke        Schornsteine
vier Stockwerke        einen Anbau

3 Draußen gibt es...
einen großen Garten
einen kleinen Garten
eine Garage

---

## b Die Zimmer        The rooms

| | |
|---|---|
| **das Zimmer (-)** } | room |
| **der Raum (¨e)** } | |
| **der Flur (-e)** | hall, landing |
| **die Diele (-n)** | hall |
| **der Gang (¨e)** | hallway, passage |
| **die Küche (-n)** | kitchen |
| **das Eßzimmer (-)** | dining-room |
| **das Wohnzimmer (-)** | living-room, drawing-room |
| **das Arbeitszimmer (-)** | study |
| **das Kinderzimmer (-)** | children's room |
| **das Schlafzimmer (-)** | bedroom |
| **das Gästezimmer (-)** | guestroom |
| **das Bad** } | bathroom |
| **das Badezimmer (-)** } | |
| **die Toilette (-n)** | toilet |
| **das Klo (-s)** | loo |

| das WC (-s) | WC |
| der Abstellraum (⸚e) | store-room, boxroom |
| der Keller (-) | cellar |
| der Dachboden (⸚) | attic |
| der Speicher (-) | loft |
| die Garage (-n) | garage |
| der Parkplatz (⸚e) | car park (*open*) |
| das Parkhaus (⸚er) | car park (*covered*) |

| oben | upstairs |
| unten | downstairs |
| ganz oben | at the very top |
| die Treppe (-n) | staircase, (flight of) stairs |
| die Stufe (-n) | one step on a staircase |

| (nicht) viel Platz | (not) a lot of room |

 See also At home: general pages 66–7.

## c Die Möbel — Furniture and equipment

| die Möbel (*pl*) | furniture |
| bewegen (*insep*) }<br>umräumen (*sep*) } | to move |

| das Fenster (-) | window |
| das Doppelfenster (-) | double glazing |
| die Verandatür (-en) | French window |
| die Schiebetür (-en) | sliding door |
| die Glasscheibe (-n) | pane of glass |
| das Fensterbrett (-er) | window sill |
| der Balkon (-s *or* -e) | balcony |
| das Rollo (-s) | (*roller*) blind |
| der Laden/Fensterladen (⸚) | shutter |
| die Gardine (-n) | (*net*) curtain |
| der Vorhang (⸚e) | (*main*) curtain |

| der Boden/Fußboden (⸚) | floor |
| die Decke (-n) | ceiling |
| die Wand (⸚e) | wall (*internal*) |
| der Teppich (-e) | carpet |
| der Teppichboden (⸚) | fitted carpet |
| die Matte (-n) | mat |

| der Schrank (¨e) | cupboard |
| das Regal (-e) | (*set of*) shelves |
| das Brett (-er) | (*individual*) shelf |
| das Bild (-er) | picture |
| das Gemälde (-) | painting |
| das Telefon (-e) | telephone |
| der Aschenbecher (-) | ash tray |
| das Papierkorb (¨e) | waste-paper basket |

See also In the kitchen, below.

### d Im Hausflur — In the hall

| die Tür (-en) | door |
| die Haustür (-en) | front door |
| das Schloß (Schlösser) | lock |
| zumachen (*sep*) | to shut |
| aufmachen (*sep*) | to open |
| schließen (er schließt) (s) | to shut |
| zuschließen (s; sep) | to lock |
| aufschließen (er schließt auf) (s; sep) | to unlock |
| der Schlüssel (-) | key |
| die Klingel (-n) | bell |
| klingeln | } to ring |
| schellen | |
| klopfen | to knock |

### e In der Küche — In the kitchen

| der Eimer (-) | bucket |
| der Abfall (¨e) | rubbish |
| der Abfalleimer (-) | waste bin |
| wegwerfen (er wirft ... weg) (s; sep) | to throw away |
| leeren | to empty |

| der Herd (-e) | cooker |
| der Gasherd (-e) | gas cooker |
| der Elektroherd (-e) | electric cooker |
| der Mikrowellenherd (-e) | microwave |
| der Backofen (¨) | oven |
| backen (er backt) (s/w mixed) | to bake |
| kochen | to cook/boil |

| | |
|---|---|
| **die Waschmaschine (-n)** | washing machine |
| **der Wäschetrockner (-)** | tumble drier |
| **die Wäsche** | washing (*ie clothes*) |
| **waschen (er wäscht) (s)** | to wash |
| **das Waschpulver** | washing powder |

| | |
|---|---|
| **spülen** ⎫ | |
| **abwaschen (er wäscht ... ab)** ⎬ | to wash up |
| **(s; sep)** ⎭ | |
| **die Spülmaschine (-n)** | dish washer |
| **das Spülmittel** | washing-up liquid |
| **das Spültuch (¨er)** ⎫ | dishcloth |
| **der Spüllappen (-)** ⎭ | |
| **das Spülbecken (-)** | sink |
| **der Hahn/Wasserhahn (¨e)** | tap |
| **aufdrehen (*sep*)** | to turn on (*tap*) |
| **abtrocknen (*sep*)** | to dry up |
| **das Geschirrtuch (¨er)** | tea-towel |

| | |
|---|---|
| **der Kühlschrank (¨e)** | fridge |
| **der Gefrierschrank (¨e)** | upright freezer |
| **die Gefriertruhe/Tiefkühltruhe (-n)** | chest freezer |
| **der Speiseschrank (¨e)** | larder, pantry |

| | |
|---|---|
| **die Schere (-n)** | pair of scissors |
| **schälen** | to peel |
| **der Kartoffelschäler (-)** | potato peeler |

| | |
|---|---|
| **das Geschirr (*no pl*)** | crockery, kitchenware |
| **fallenlassen (er läßt ... fallen) (s)** | to drop |
| **aus Versehen** | by accident |
| **das Glas (¨er)** | glass, jar |
| **die Obstschale (-n)** | fruit-bowl |
| **die Schüssel (-n)** | dish, bowl |
| **die Kanne (-n)** ⎫ | jug |
| **das Kännchen (-)** ⎭ | |
| **füllen** | to fill |
| **die Teekanne (-n)** | teapot |
| **die Kaffeekanne (-n)** | coffee pot |
| **die Kaffeemaschine (-n)** | coffee maker |
| **die Milchkanne (-n)** | milk jug |
| **der Topf (¨e)** | pot, saucepan |
| **der Kochtopf (¨e)** | saucepan |
| **der Schnellkochtopf (¨e)** | pressure cooker |

| die Kasserolle (-n) | saucepan |
| die Pfanne/Bratpfanne (-n) | frying-pan |
| der Wasserkocher (-) | kettle |
| der Mixer (-) | blender |
| der Toaster (-) | toaster |
| die Waage (-n) | (set of) scales |
| die Dose (-n) | tin, can |
| der Dosenöffner (-) | tin opener |
| aufmachen (sep) | to open |
| der Korken (-) | cork |
| der Korkenzieher (-) | corkscrew |
| die Flasche (-n) | bottle |
| der Flaschenöffner (-) | bottle opener |
| die Serviette (-n) | serviette, napkin |
| der Strohhalm/Trinkhalm (-e) | drinking straw |
| der Hocker (-) | stool |

 See also Cutlery and crockery, pages 35–6.

## f Im Wohnzimmer und Eßzimmer
## In the living-room and dining-room

| der Tisch (-e) | table |
| der Eßtisch (-e) | dining-table |
| den Tisch decken | to lay the table |
| (den Tisch) abräumen (*sep*) | to clear away |
| aus Holz (*n*) | made of wood |
| die Tischdecke (-n) | table cloth |
| das Tablett (-e *or* -s) | tray |

| der Stuhl (¨e) | chair (*without arms*) |
| der Lehnstuhl (¨e) }<br>der Sessel (-) } | armchair |
| Platz nehmen (er nimmt) (*s*) | to take a seat |
| das Sofa (-s) | sofa, settee |
| die Couch (-es *or* -en) | couch |
| das Kissen (-) | cushion |

| der Hi-Fi-Turm (¨e) | hi-fi stack |
| die Stereoanlage (-n) | stereo system |
| der Plattenspieler (-) | record-player, turntable |
| das Radio (-s) | radio |
| Radio hören | to listen to the radio |
| das Transistorradio (-s) | transistor radio |

| | |
|---|---|
| der Lautsprecher (-) <br> die Box (-en) | loudspeaker |
| der Fernseher (-) <br> der Fernsehapparat (-e) | television set |
| fernsehen (er sieht fern) (*s; sep*) | to watch TV |
| das Fernsehen | TV (*the medium*) |
| im Fernsehen | on TV |
| im Radio | on the radio |
| der Videorecorder (-) | video (recorder) |
| die Videokassette (-n) | video cassette |
| das Büfett (-s *or* -e) <br> die Anrichte (-n) | sideboard |
| das Bücherregal (-e) | bookshelves |
| der Bücherschrank (-e) | bookcase |
| der Couchtisch (-e) | coffee-table |
| der Arbeitstisch (-e) | desk |
| die Schreibmaschine (-n) | typewriter |
| der Computer (-) | computer |
| die Tischlampe (-n) | table-lamp |
| die Stehlampe (-n) | standard lamp |
| der Strahler (-) | spotlight |
| die Pflanze (-n) | plant |
| die Vase (-n) | vase |
| die Nippsachen (*pl*) | ornaments |
| die Uhr (-en) | clock |
| die Kuckucksuhr (-en) | cuckoo-clock |
| die Kerze (-n) | candle |
| das Feuer | fire |
| der Kamin (-e) | fireplace |
| die Kohle (-n) | coal |
| der Gasofen (-) | gas fire |
| der elektrische Heizofen (-) | electric fire |
| anzünden (*sep*) | to light |
| sich entspannen (*insep*) | to relax |

## g Im Schlafzimmer / In the bedroom

| | |
|---|---|
| das Bett (-en) | bed |
| die Matratze (-n) | mattress |
| das Kopfkissen (-) | pillow |
| die Bettwäsche <br> das Bettzeug | bed linen |

| | |
|---|---|
| die Decke (-n) | blanket |
| das Federbett (-en) | duvet |
| die Steppdecke (-n) | quilt |
| das Laken (-) } das Bettuch (¨er) | sheet |
| die Heizdecke (-n) | electric blanket |
| der Nachttisch (-e) | bedside table |
| die Nachttischlampe (-en) | bedside light |
| der Wecker (-) | alarm clock |
| der Radiowecker (-) | radio alarm clock |
| den Wecker auf 7 Uhr stellen | to set the alarm for 7 o'clock |
| die Kommode (-n) | chest of drawers |
| die Schublade (-n) | drawer |
| die Frisierkommode (-n) | dressing table |
| die Kleiderbürste (-n) | clothes brush |
| der Spiegel (-) | mirror |
| der Kleiderschrank (¨e) | wardrobe |
| das Poster (-) | poster |
| das Spielzeug | toy/toys |
| die Puppe (-n) | doll |
| aufräumen (*sep*) | to clear up |
| seine Sachen wegräumen (*sep*) | to tidy away one's things |
| in Ordnung halten (er hält) (*s*) | to keep tidy |
| teilen | to share |

See also Before School, pages 11–12.

## h Im Badezimmer — In the bathroom

| | |
|---|---|
| das Badezimmer } das Bad | bathroom |
| die Badewanne (-n) | bath (tub) |
| (sich) baden } ein Bad nehmen (er nimmt) (*s*) | to have a bath |
| die Dusche (-n) | shower |
| (sich) duschen | to have a shower |
| das Waschbecken (-) | basin |
| das Bidet (-s) | bidet |
| die Seife | soap |
| der Schwamm (¨e) | sponge |
| der Waschlappen (-) | flannel |
| das Handtuch (¨er) | towel |
| das Badetuch (¨er) | bath towel |

| sich rasieren | to shave |
| der (elektrische) Rasierapparat (-e) | (electric) rasor |
| der Rasierschaum | shaving foam |
| sich (Dat) die Zähne bürsten/putzen | to brush/clean one's teeth |
| ich putze mir die Zähne | I brush my teeth |
| die Zahnbürste (-n) | toothbrush |
| die Zahnpasta | toothpaste |
| die Tube (-n) | tube |
| die Toilette (-n) | toilet |
| auf die Toilette gehen* / aufs Klo gehen* | to go to the toilet |
| das Toilettenpapier | toilet paper |

 See also Before School, pages 11–12 for more bathroom vocabulary.

## Jetzt bist du dran! 25

*Schreib, was du in diesen Bildern siehst!*

*Write down what you can see in these pictures.*

## Jetzt bist du dran! 26

*Die Buchstaben bilden den Namen von etwas im Haus auf deutsch.*

*The letters when unjumbled spell things in the home. They are all single words.*

➡

| | | | |
|---|---|---|---|
| 1 CUTE ROMP | der _ _ _ _ _ _ _ _ | (Im Büro und oft zu Hause) |
| 2 PAPA RAT | der _ _ _ _ _ _ _ | (Maschine) |
| 3 PEG LIES | der _ _ _ _ _ _ _ | (Im Bad und im Schlafzimmer) |
| 4 NUT SEESTAR | die _ _ _ _ _ _ _ _ _ | (In der Kommode) |
| 5 SHADE CLUB | die _ _ _ _ _ _ _ _ _ | (Unter dem Tisch) |
| 6 NEAT RICH | die _ _ _ _ _ _ _ | (Möbelstück im Eßzimmer) |
| 7 BAN WEE DAN | die _ _ _ _ _ _ _ _ _ | (Im Bad) |
| 8 PREACHER LUST | der _ _ _ _ _ _ _ _ _ _ _ _ | (Gehört zur Stereoanlage) |
| 9 RED GASH | der _ _ _ _ _ _ _ | (In der Küche) |
| 10 BUS ATE SUGAR | der _ _ _ _ _ _ _ _ _ _ | (Zum Saubermachen) |

## i Hausarbeit — Chores

| | |
|---|---|
| der Haushalt (-e) | household |
| putzen ⎫ saubermachen (sep) ⎬ | to clean |
| aufräumen (sep) | to tidy up |
| abstauben (sep) ⎫ Staub wischen ⎬ | to dust |
| fegen | to sweep |
| der Besen (-) | broom |
| der Staubsauger (-) | vacuum cleaner |
| staubsaugen (sep) | to vacuum |
| spülen ⎫ abwaschen (er wäscht ... ab) (s; sep) ⎬ | to wash up |
| abtrocknen | to dry up |
| den Müll hinaustragen (s; sep) | to take out the rubbish |
| die Mülltonne (-n) | dustbin |
| kochen | to cook |
| Gemüse schälen | to peel vegetables |
| den Tisch decken | to lay the table |
| den Tisch abräumen (sep) | to clear the table |
| bügeln | to iron |
| das Bügeleisen (-) | iron |
| das Bügelbrett (-er) | ironing board |
| die Nähmaschine (-n) | sewing machine |

| | |
|---|---|
| nähen | to sew |
| flicken | to mend (clothes) |
| das Bett machen | to make the bed |
| die Putzfrau (-en) | cleaning lady |
| | |
| das Heimwerken | odd jobs, DIY |
| der Pinsel (-) | paint brush |
| streichen/anstreichen | |
| (er streicht ... an) (s; sep) | to paint |
| 'Frisch gestrichen' | 'Wet paint' |
| tapezieren | to wallpaper |
| der Hammer (¨) | hammer |
| der Nagel (¨) | nail |
| die Schraube (-n) | screw |
| der Schraubenzieher (-) | screwdriver |
| der Schraubenschlüssel (-) | spanner |
| die Leiter (-n) | ladder |
| der Klempner (-) | plumber |
| | |
| anbauen (sep) | to build an extension |
| der Anbau (-ten) | extension |
| reparieren | to repair |

## j Heizung und Beleuchtung    Heating and lighting

| | |
|---|---|
| der Elektriker (-) | electrician |
| funktionieren | to work, function |
| die Zentralheizung | central heating |
| heizen | to heat |
| der Heizkörper (-) | radiator |
| der offene Kamin | fire (in grate) |
| brennen (w irreg) | to burn |
| die Kohle (-n) | coal |
| das Holz | wood |
| | |
| das Licht (-er) | light |
| die Lampe (-n) | lamp |
| der Lampenschirm (-e) | lamp-shade |
| die Birne (-n) | bulb |
| das Licht ist an/aus | the light is on/off |
| anmachen (sep) }<br>einschalten (sep) } | to switch on |
| ausmachen (sep) }<br>ausschalten (sep) } | to switch off |

| der Schalter (-) | switch |
| der Knopf (⏀e) | button |
| (auf) den Knopf drücken | to press the button |
| die Steckdose (-n) | electric socket |
| der Stecker (-) | plug |
| elektrisch | electric(al) |
| der Apparat (-e) | appliance, gadget |
| benutzen | to use |
| kaputt | broken |

See also In the kitchen, pages 70–2.

## k Der Garten (⏀) The garden

| der Hof (⏀e) | yard, courtyard |
| die Terrasse (-n) | patio |

| das Gras | grass |
| der Rasen | lawn |
| die Wiese (-n) | lawn/meadow |
| mähen | to mow |
| der Rasenmäher (-) | lawn-mower |
| die Gartenarbeit machen | to garden |
| das Unkraut (*sg only*) | weeds |
| Unkraut jäten | to do the weeding |
| die Pflanze (-n) | plant |
| pflanzen | to plant |
| wachsen* (er wächst) (s) | to grow (*intransitive*) |
| züchten | to grow, cultivate |
| gießen (er gießt) (s) | to water |
| die Blume (-n) | flower |
| das Blumenbeet (-e) | flower bed |
| die Rose (-n) | rose |
| der Baum (⏀e) | tree |
| der Obstbaum (⏀e) | fruit tree |
| der Busch (⏀e) | bush |

| der Weg (-e) | path |
| die Mauer (-n) | wall (*external*) |
| der Schuppen (-) | shed |
| die Hütte (-n) | hut |
| das Gartenhaus (⏀er) | summer house |
| die Bank (⏀e) | bench |
| der Liegestuhl (⏀e) | deckchair |

| | |
|---|---|
| **der Sonnenschirm (-e)** | sunshade |
| **der Gartenstuhl (¨e)** | garden chair |
| **der Swimming-pool (-s)** | (garden) swimming pool |
| **der Tennisplatz (¨e)** | tennis court |
| **die Aussicht (-en) (auf...)** | view (of...) |

## Jetzt bist du dran! 27

*Wohin gehören die Sachen im Haus?*

*Where do things belong in the house?*

| | | | |
|---|---|---|---|
| Der Flaschenöffner | | neben den Hutständer | im Schlafzimmer. |
| Die CDs | | auf den Nachttisch | auf dem Dachboden. |
| Die Schirme | | an die Wand | im Eßzimmer. |
| Der Wecker | gehört | in die Ecke | auf dem Flur. |
| Der Rasenmäher | | auf den Stuhl | in der Garage. |
| Meine Pullover | gehören | auf das Regal | in der Küche. |
| Das Haarspray | | in die Schublade | im Bad. |
| Unsere Koffer | | in den Kühlschrank | im Gästezimmer. |
| Das Besteck | | auf den Tisch | im Garten. |
| Die Fotos vom Urlaub | | neben den Fernseher | im Keller. |
| Die Kaffeemaschine | | usw. | |

## I Haustiere — Pets

| | |
|---|---|
| **das Haustier (-e)** | pet |
| **behalten (*insep*)** | to keep, look after |
| **der Hund (-e)** | dog |
| **den Hund ausführen (*sep*)** | to walk the dog |
| **an der Leine** | on the lead |
| **die Hundehütte (-n)** | kennel |
| **bellen** | to bark |
| **wau wau** | woof-woof |
| **'Vorsicht, bissiger Hund'** | 'Beware of the dog' |
| **leg dich!** **Platz!** | lie down |
| **die Katze (-n)** | cat |
| **miau/miauen** | miaow/to miaow |
| **schnurren** | to purr |

| | |
|---|---|
| **der Käfig (-e)** | cage |
| **das Kaninchen (-)** | rabbit |
| **der Fisch/Goldfisch (-e)** | (gold)fish |

| | |
|---|---|
| **der Hamster (-)** | hamster |
| **das Meerschweinchen (-)** | guinea-pig |
| **die Maus (Mäuse)** | mouse |
| **die Ratte (-n)** | rat |
| **die Schildkröte (-n)** | tortoise/turtle |
| **die Schlange (-n)** | snake |
| **das Pferd (-e)** | horse |
| **das Pony (-s)** | pony |
| **der Stall (¨e)** | stable, hutch |
| **der Vogel (¨)** | bird |
| **der Wellensittich (-e)** | budgerigar |
| **das Insekt (-en)** | insect |
| **das Futter** | food |
| **füttern** | to feed |
| **fressen (er frißt) (s)** | to eat (*animals eating*) |

# Jetzt bist du dran! 28

*Füll das Kreuzworträtsel aus!*       *Fill in the crossword puzzle.*

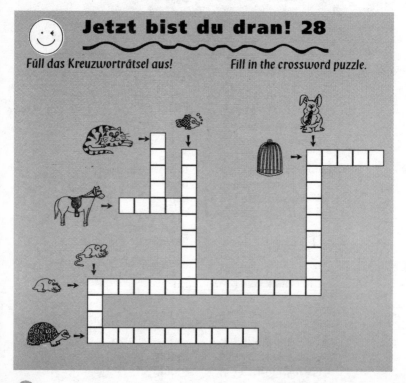

### 3 Freizeit
### Free time and social activities

#### a Hobbys und Beschäftigungen
#### Hobbies and activities

| | |
|---|---|
| sich (gut) amüsieren | to have fun, enjoy oneself |
| das Hobby (-s) | hobby |
| das Interesse (-n) | interest |
| die Freizeitbeschäftigung (-en) | leisure activity |
| verschieden | different, various |
| das macht Spaß | that's fun |
| das macht mir Spaß | I enjoy that |
| viel Spaß! | have fun! |
| ich (+verb) gern | I enjoy ...ing |
| ich (+verb) leidenschaftlich gern | I am mad about ...ing |
| versuchen | to attempt, try |
| sonst nichts | nothing else |

#### b Ausgehen
#### Going out

| | |
|---|---|
| treffen (er trifft) (s) | to meet |
| begegnen* (+Dat) (insep) | to meet (by accident), run into |
| der Treffpunkt (-e) | meeting place |
| (sich) verabreden (insep) | to make an arrangement |
| die Verabredung (-en) | arrangement, date |
| vorschlagen (er schlägt ... vor) (s; sep) | to suggest |
| besprechen (er bespricht) (s; insep) | to discuss (transitive) |
| beschließen (er beschließt) (s; insep) | to decide |
| ausgehen* (mit...) (er geht aus) (s; sep) | to go out (with...) |
| weggehen* (er geht ... weg) (s; sep) | to go out, leave |
| mitmachen (sep) | to join in (an activity) |
| zu Hause bleiben* (er bleibt) (s) | to stay at home |
| Einkaufen gehen* (s) | to go shopping |
| die Gelegenheit (-en) <br> die Chance (-n) } | chance, opportunity |
| klappen | to work out, go smoothly |

| | |
|---|---|
| der Freund (-e) | friend (*m*)/boyfriend |
| die Freundin (-nen) | friend (*f*)/girlfriend |
| die Clique (-n) | gang |
| die Gesellschaft (-en) | company/society |
| sich unterhalten (er unterhält sich) (*s; insep*) | to chat |
| die Unterhaltung (-en) | chat |
| plaudern | to chat |
| reden | to speak |
| anquatschen (*sep*) | to chat up |
| hast du Lust? | do you want to? |
| ich habe keine Lust | I don't want to |
| hau ab! | push off! get lost! |
| sich schön anziehen (er zieht sich ... an) (*s; sep*) | to dress up |
| sich schminken | to put on make-up |
| spannend | exciting |
| Verwandte besuchen (*insep*) | to visit relations |
| der Besuch (-e) | visit/visitor |
| wir bekommen Besuch | we've got visitors coming |

## Jetzt bist du dran! 29

*Verbinde die zwei Hälften der Sätze.*

Join up the two halves of the sentences.

| | |
|---|---|
| Hast du Lust, | etwas Interessantes vor. |
| Was hast du eigentlich | all mein Taschengeld ausgegeben. |
| Willst du nachher | für die Aufführung schon gekauft. |
| Ich lade dich | des Semesters feiern. |
| Udo ist langweilig; er macht | heute abend ja zu! |
| Ich habe die Karten | sehr empfohlen. |
| Ich schlage | mit mir ins Konzert zu gehen? |
| Wir wollen zusammen das Ende | unbedingt die Haare waschen! |
| Ich habe aber leider schon | zu einer Fete bei Heinz ein. |
| Die Disco in der Talstraße hat | nie mit! |
| Marianne hat mir den Film | Freitag abend vor? |
| Ich muß mir aber | ins China-Restaurant? |

## c Die Unterhaltung — Entertainment

|  |  |
|---|---|
| **die Veranstaltung (-en)** | organised event |
| **der Ausflug (¨e)** | excursion |
| **der Klub/Jugendklub (-s)** | (youth) club |
| **das Jugendzentrum (-zentren)** ⎫ **das Haus der Jugend** ⎭ | youth centre |
| **der Verein (-e)** ⎫ **der Klub (-s)** ⎭ | club |
| **die Party (-s)** ⎫ **die Fete (-n)** ⎭ | party |
| **die Feier (-n)** | celebration, party |
| **feiern** | to celebrate |
| **einladen (er lädt ... ein) (s; sep)** | to invite |
| **jemanden einladen** | to pay for s.o. |
| **ich lade dich zu einer Cola ein** | I'll buy you a coke |
| **bezahlen (insep)** | to pay (for...) |
| **teuer** | expensive |
| **billig** | cheap |
| **kostenlos** ⎫ **gratis** ⎭ | free |
| **der Nachtklub (-s)** | night-club |
| **die Disco/Disko/Diskothek** | disco |
| **tanzen** | to dance |
| **die Kneipe (-n)** ⎫ **die Gaststätte (-n)** ⎪ **das Lokal (-e)** ⎬ **die Wirtschaft (-en)** ⎭ | pub |
| **die Bar (-s)** | bar, night-club |
| **die Schenke (-n)** | inn, tavern |
| **der Stammtisch (-e)** | table for regulars in pub |
| **der Weinkeller (-)** ⎫ **die Weinstube (-n)** ⎭ | wine-bar |
| **die Weinprobe (-n)** | wine-tasting |
| **der Ratskeller (-)** | townhall restaurant |
| **das Kasino (-s)** | casino |
| **spielen** | to gamble |
| **der Würfel (-)** | die |
| **das Würfelspiel (-e)** | dice games |
| **um Geld** | for money |
| **Karten spielen** | to play cards |

| | |
|---|---|
| die Lotterie (-n) | lottery |
| das Rubbellos | scratch-card |
| der Karneval (-s) | carnival |
| der Jahrmarkt (¨e) }<br>die Kirmes (-sen) } | funfair |

## d Sport — Sport

| | |
|---|---|
| der Sport (Sportarten) | sport |
| sportlich | sporty |
| (viel) Sport treiben (er treibt) (s) | to do (a lot of) sport |
| die Mannschaft (-en) | team |
| das Mitglied (-er) | member |
| das Spiel (-e) | game, match |
| der Spieler (-) }<br>die Spielerin (-nen) } | player (*m/f*) |
| der Sportler (-) }<br>die Sportlerin (-nen) } | sportsman/woman, athlete (*m/f*) |
| der Profi (-s) | professional player |
| der Amateur (-e) | amateur |
| der Teilnehmer (-) | participant (*m*) |
| die Teilnehmerin (-nen) | participant (*f*) |
| der Verein (-e) | club |
| der Zuschauer (-) | spectator |
| der Fan (-s) | fan |
| rufen (er ruft) (s) | to call, shout |
| schreien (er schreit) (s) | to shout, yell |
| der Punkt (-e) | point, mark |
| das Glück | (good) luck |
| das Ergebnis (-se) | result |
| das Tor (-e) | goal |
| ein Tor schießen (er schießt) (s) | to score a goal |
| wie steht's? | what's the score? |
| es steht eins zu null | the score is 1–0 |
| das Spiel war unentschieden | the match was a draw |
| gewinnen (er gewinnt) (s; *insep*) | to win |
| der Pokal (-e) | cup |
| der Sieger (-)/die Siegerin (-nen) | winner (*m/f*) |
| schlagen (er schlägt) (s) | to beat |
| verlieren (gegen jemand)<br>(er verliert) (s; *insep*) | to lose (to someone) |
| der Verlierer (-) | loser (*m*) |
| die Verliererin (-nen) | loser (*f*) |

| | |
|---|---|
| die Saison (-s) | season |
| die (Welt)Meisterschaft (-en) | (world) championship |
| die erste Runde | the first round |
| das Endspiel (-e) | final |
| das Finale | final(s) |
| die Olympischen Spiele (*pl*) | Olympic Games |
| | |
| der Sportplatz ("e) | sportsground |
| das Stadion (Stadien) | stadium |
| das Feld (-er) | field/pitch |
| das Sportzentrum (-zentren) | sports centre |
| das Fitneßzentrum (-zentren) | fitness centre |
| der Umkleideraum ("e) | changing-room |
| trainieren | to train, to practise |
| sich trimmen | to do keep-fit exercises |
| fit werden* (er wird) (s) | to get fit |
| fit bleiben* (er bleibt) (s) | to stay fit |
| anstrengend | strenuous |
| ermüdend | tiring |
| | |
| Fußball | football |
| die Bundesliga | German football league |
| Rugby | rugby |
| Hockey | hockey |
| Netzball | netball |
| Handball | handball |
| Volleyball | volleyball |
| Basketball | basketball |
| Laufen | running |
| die Leichtathletik | athletics |
| rennen* (er rennt) (*irreg w*) | to run |
| der Hundertmeterlauf | the 100 metres (*race*) |
| springen* (er springt) (s) | to jump |
| Geländelauf machen | to do cross-country running |
| joggen | to jog |
| Joggen/Jogging | jogging |
| der Hochsprung | high jump |
| der Dreisprung | triple jump |
| der Weitsprung | long jump |
| der Hürdenlauf | hurdling |
| der Staffellauf | relay race |
| den Speer werfen (er wirft) (s) | to throw the javelin |
| den Diskus werfen (s) | to throw the discus |
| Reiten | horse-riding |

| | |
|---|---|
| reiten* (er reitet) (s) | to go horse-riding, to ride |
| das Fahrrad/Rad (¨er) | bicycle |
| radfahren* (er fährt Rad) (s; sep) | to ride a bicycle |
| das Mountain-Bike (-s) | mountain-bike |
| eine Radtour machen | to go on a bike tour |
| die Rollschuhbahn (-en) | roller-skating rink |
| Rollschuh laufen* (er läuft) (s) | to go roller-skating |
| das Skateboard (-s) | skateboard |

| | |
|---|---|
| der Wassersport | water sports |
| Schwimmen | swimming |
| schwimmen* (er schwimmt) (s) | to swim |
| baden | to swim (more leisurely) |
| das Schwimmbad (¨er) | swimming pool |
| das Hallenbad (¨er) | indoor swimming pool |
| das Freibad (¨er) | open-air swimming pool |
| der Badeanzug (¨e) | swimsuit |
| die Badehose (-n) | swimming trunks |
| die Bademütze (-n) | swimming cap |
| das Badetuch (¨er) | swimming towel |
| das Sprungbrett (-er) | diving board |
| einen Kopfsprung machen | to dive |
| tauchen | to duck/swim under water |
| Wasserball | water polo |
| segeln | to sail |
| Segeln | sailing |
| das Boot/das Segelboot (-e) | (sailing) boat |
| das Segelflugzeug (-e) | glider |
| Windsurfen | windsurfing |
| das Surfbrett (-er) | surfboard |
| rudern | to row |
| Rudern | rowing |

| | |
|---|---|
| Turnen | gymnastics |
| die Turnhalle (-n) | gymnasium |
| tanzen | to dance |
| der Tanzsaal (-säle) | dance-hall |
| Gewichtheben | weightlifting |
| das Training/Fitneßtraining | training |
| der Trainingsanzug (¨e) | track-suit |

| | |
|---|---|
| Tennis/Tischtennis | tennis/table-tennis |
| die Tischtennisplatte (-n) | table-tennis table |
| Federball/Badminton | badminton |

| der Schläger (-) | bat, racket |
|---|---|
| das Netz (-e) | net |
| kegeln | to go bowling |
| die Kegelbahn (-en) | bowling alley |
| angeln | to fish |
| Angeln | fishing |
| die Angelrute (-n) | fishing rod |
| fangen (er fängt) (s) | to catch |

 For Winter sports, see pages 108–9.

## Jetzt bist du dran! 30

*Schau dir die Bilder an! Findest du heraus, welches Wort in die Lücke gehört?*

*Look at the pictures. Can you find the missing words.*

1 Ich spiele gern .................. und ..................

2 Ich mag auch gern ..................

3 Meine Schwester läuft gern ..................

4 Mein Freund spielt gern ..................

5 Am Wochenende gehe ich gern in eine ..................

| **e Im Freien** | **In the open air** |
|---|---|
| draußen | outside |
| der Pfadfinder (-) | scout |
| die Pfadfinderin (-nen) | guide |
| der Park (-s) | park |
| die Parkanlage (-n) | park, gardens |
| 'Betreten des Rasens verboten' | 'Keep off the grass' |
| wandern* | to hike, ramble |

| | |
|---|---|
| **die Wanderung (-en)** | hike, ramble |
| **spazierengehen** | |
| **(er geht ... spazieren)** (*s; sep*) | to go for a walk |
| **sich bewegen** (*insep*) | to take some exercise |
| **der Spaziergang (˝e)** | walk, stroll |
| **klettern\*** | to climb |
| **bergsteigen gehen\*** (*s*) | to go mountain climbing |
| **der Wegweiser (-)** | signpost |

| | |
|---|---|
| **das Picknick (-s)** | picnic |
| **Picknick machen** | to have a picnic |
| **die Thermosflasche ®** | thermos flask ® |
| **grillen** | to barbecue |
| **der Grill (-s)** | grill, barbecue |
| **das Grillfest (-e)** | barbecue (*event*) |
| **die Grillplatte (-n)** | platter of barbecued meats |

See also Scenery, page 117 and Animals, birds and insects, pages 118–20.

## f Die Musik — Music

| | |
|---|---|
| **Musik hören** | to listen to music |
| **CDs/Kassetten zuhören** | to listen to CDs/cassettes |
| **laut** | loud(ly) |
| **leise** | soft(ly) |
| **der Rock** | rock music |
| **der Pop/die Popmusik** | pop music |
| **der Jazz** | jazz |
| **der Rap** | rap |
| **die Volksmusik** | folk music |
| **die klassische Musik** | classical music |

| | |
|---|---|
| **der Hit (-s)** | hit |
| **die Hitparade** | charts |
| **die Gruppe (-n)** | group |
| **die Band (-s)** | band, group (*less official*) |
| **die Platte/Schallplatte (-n)** | record |
| **die Langspielplatte (-n)** | LP |
| **die Single** | single |
| **das Tonband (˝er)** | (recording) tape |
| **das Tonbandgerät (-e)** | tape recorder |

| | |
|---|---|
| aufnehmen (er nimmt ... auf) (*s; sep*) | to record |
| die (Video)aufnahme (-n) | (video) recording |
| die Kassette (-n) | cassette |
| der Kassettenrecorder (-) | cassette player |
| der Walkman (-s) | walkman |
| die CD (-s) | CD |
| der CD-Player (-) | CD player |
| der Discman | CD walkman |
| der Chor (¨e) | choir |
| singen (er singt) (*s*) | to sing |
| der Sänger (-) die Sängerin (-nen) } | singer (*m/f*) |
| das Orchester (-) | orchestra |
| die Kapelle/Blaskapelle (-n) | (brass) band |
| das Konzert (-e) | concert |
| das Mitglied (-er) | member |
| der Musiker (-) die Musikerin (-nen) } | musician (*m/f*) |
| der Dirigent die Dirigentin (-nen) } | conductor (*m/f*) |
| der Solist/die Solistin (-nen) | soloist (*m/f*) |
| spielen | to play |
| das Instrument (-e) | instrument |
| das Klavier | piano |
| die Flöte (-n) | flute |
| die Blockflöte (-n) | recorder |
| die Klarinette (-n) | clarinet |
| die Oboe (-n) | oboe |
| die Trompete (-n) | trumpet |
| die Geige (-n)/die Violine (-n) | violin |
| die Gitarre (-n) | guitar |
| das Schlagzeug | drums, drum-kit |
| das Saxophon (-e) | saxophone |
| der Anfänger (-) die Anfängerin (-nen) } | beginner (*m/f*) |

## g Die Kunst (¨e)    Art

| | |
|---|---|
| das Museum (Museen) | museum |
| die Kunstgalerie | art gallery |
| die Ausstellung (-en) | exhibition |

| | |
|---|---|
| **besichtigen** | to visit, have a look round |
| **die Besichtigung (-en)** | visit, tour |

| | |
|---|---|
| **das Gemälde (-)** | painting |
| **der Maler (-)/die Malerin (-nen)** | painter (*m/f*) |
| **malen** | to paint |
| **die Zeichnung (-en)** | drawing |
| **zeichnen** | to draw |
| **das Bild (-er)** | picture |
| **das Porträt (-s)** | portrait |
| **das Stilleben (-)** | still life |
| **die Landschaft (-en)** | landscape painting |
| **im Vordergrund/Hintergrund** | in the foreground/background |
| **die Skulptur (-en)** | sculpture |
| **die Statue (-n)** | statue |

## h Lesen — Reading

| | |
|---|---|
| **lesen (er liest) (*s*)** | to read |
| **das Buch (¨-er)** | book |
| **der Roman (-e)** | novel |
| **der Krimi (-s)** | thriller, detective novel |
| **die Geschichte (-n)** | story |
| **der Autor (-en)/die Autorin (-nen)** | author (*m/f*) |
| **das Gedicht (-e)** | poem |
| **der Dichter (-)** | poet |
| **das Taschenbuch (¨-er)** | paperback |
| **der Verlag (-e)** | publisher (*company*) |

| | |
|---|---|
| **die Beschreibung (-en)** | description |
| **der Titel (-)** | title |
| **der Held (-en, -en)** | hero |
| **die Heldin (-nen)** | heroine |
| **die Figur (-en)** | character |
| **wahr** | true |
| **erfunden** | imaginary |
| **ergreifend** | moving |

## i Andere Hobbys — Other hobbies

| | |
|---|---|
| **basteln** | to make models etc |
| **kleben** | to stick |
| **die Sammlung (-en)** | collection |

| | |
|---|---|
| **sammeln** | to collect |
| **der Aufkleber (-)** | sticker |
| **das Abzeichen (-)** | badge |
| **das Stadtwappen (-)** | city coat-of-arms |
| **Karten spielen** | to play cards |
| **das Brettspiel (-e)** | board-game |
| **das Glücksspiel (-e)** | game of chance |
| **(das) Schach** | chess |
| | |
| **nähen** | to sew |
| **die Nadel (-n)** | needle |
| **stricken** | to knit |
| | |
| **die Fotografie** | photography |
| **(schwarzweiß) fotografieren** | to take (black-and-white) photographs |
| **knipsen** | to take snaps |
| **die Aufnahme (-n)** | picture/recording |
| **das Foto (-s)** | photo |
| **der Farbfilm (-e)** | colour film |
| **das Dia (-s)** | slide, transparency |
| **der Fotoapparat (-e)** | camera |
| **der Videorecorder (-)** | camcorder |
| **Theater spielen** | to act in plays |
| **das Schauspiel (-e)** | play |
| **aufführen (*sep*)** | to put on (*a play*) |
| | |
| **nichts tun (er tut) (*s*)** | to do nothing |
| **(sich) ausschlafen** | |
| **(er schläft aus) (*s; sep*)** | to sleep in late |

## j Die Presse     The press

| | |
|---|---|
| **die Zeitung (-en)** | newspaper |
| **die Zeitschrift (-en)** | magazine, periodical |
| **die Boulevardzeitung (-en)** | tabloid newspaper |
| **das Magazin (-e)** | (news) magazine |
| **die Illustrierte (*f adj. noun*)** | magazine |
| **die Wochenendbeilage (-n)** | weekend supplement |
| **das Feuilleton** | cultural feature section |
| **die Seite (-n)** | page |
| **der Artikel (-)** | article |
| **die Schlagzeile (-n)** | headline |
| **die Sportseite (-n)** | sports page |

| | |
|---|---|
| das **Kreuzworträtsel** (-) | crossword |
| die **Kleinanzeige** (-n) | small ad |
| die **Karikatur** (-en) | cartoon |
| der **Comic** (-s) | comic strip |
| das **Comic-Heft** (-e) | comic |
| **lustig** | funny |
| **seriös** | serious |
| **aktuell** | topical |

| | |
|---|---|
| die **Nachricht** (-en) | news |
| die **Neuigkeit** (-en) | news item |
| die **Politik** (*no pl*) | politics |
| die **Wirtschaft** | economy |
| das **Ereignis** (-se) | event |
| **geschehen*** (es geschieht) (s) | to happen |
| einen **Kommentar abgeben** (zu) | to comment (on) |
| die **Umfrage** (-n) | survey |

## k Radio und Fernsehen        Radio and television

| | |
|---|---|
| das **Radio** (-s) | radio |
| der **Rundfunk** | radio (*the medium*) |
| das **Autoradio** (-s) | car radio |
| der **(Stereo)empfänger** (-) | (stereo) receiver |
| die **Kurzwelle/Mittelwelle/** **Langwelle** | short/medium/long wave |
| die **Ultrakurzwelle** (UKW) | VHF |
| **Radio hören** | to listen to the radio |
| der **Ansager** (-) | announcer (m) |
| die **Ansagerin** (-nen) | announcer (f) |
| der **Zuhörer** (-) | listener |
| der **Zuschauer** (-) | viewer |
| **anschalten** **einschalten** (*sep*) } | to switch on |
| **ausschalten** (*sep*) | to switch off |
| **umschalten** (*sep*) | to change programmes |
| die **Antenne** (-n) | aerial |
| **fernsehen** (er sieht ... fern) (s; sep) | to watch TV |
| der **Fernseher** (-) | television set |
| **senden** | to broadcast |
| die **Sendung** (-en) | programme |
| das **Programm** (-e) | channel, programmes |
| die **Folge** (-n) | episode |

| | |
|---|---|
| die Sendereihe (-n) | series |
| die Fortsetzung (-en) | instalment |
| die Nachrichten (*pl*) | news |
| die Wettervorhersage (-n) | weather forecast |
| der Dokumentarfilm (-e) | documentary |
| die Seifenoper (-n) | soap opera |
| die Spielshow (-s) | game show |
| das Quiz (-) | quiz show |
| der Fernsehfilm (-e) | film produced for TV |
| der Spielfilm (-e) | film produced for cinema |
| die Sportsendung (-en) | sports programme |
| die Werbung (-en) ⎫<br>der Werbespot/Spot (-s) ⎬ | advertisement |
| die Satellitenschüssel (-n) | satellite receiver dish |
| das Kabelfernsehen | cable TV |
| die Fernbedienung (-en) | remote control |

## ❙ Das Kino (-s) — Cinema

| | |
|---|---|
| der Eingang (⁻e) | entrance |
| der Ausgang (⁻e) | exit |
| der Notausgang (⁻e) | emergency exit |
| die Kasse (-n) | box office |
| der Eintritt | entry |
| das Eintrittsgeld | admission |
| die Eintrittskarte (-n) | ticket |
| die Karten besorgen (*insep*) | to buy the tickets |
| der Platz (⁻e) | seat |
| die Reihe (-n) | row |
| das Parkett | stalls |
| der Rang ⎫<br>der Balkon ⎬ | circle |
| der Bildschirm (-e) | screen |

| | |
|---|---|
| der Filmstar (-s) | film star |
| der Regisseur (-e) ⎫<br>die Regisseurin (-nen) ⎬ | director (*m/f*) |
| der Produktionsleiter (-) ⎫<br>die Produktionsleiterin (-nen) ⎪<br>der Produzent (-en) ⎬<br>die Produzentin (-nen) ⎭ | producer (*m/f*) |
| der Film (-e) | film |
| der Zeichentrickfilm (-e) | cartoon |
| der Wildwestfilm (-e) | western |

| | |
|---|---|
| der Horrorfilm (-e) | horror film |
| die Filmkomödie (-n) | comedy |
| die Vorschau (-en) | preview, trailer |
| der Farbfilm (-e) | film in colour |
| der Schwarzweißfilm (-e) | black-and-white film |
| mit Untertiteln | with subtitles |
| synchronisiert | dubbed |

## m Das Theater (-)     Theatre

| | |
|---|---|
| das Theaterstück (-e) | play |
| der Schauspieler (-) | actor |
| die Schauspielerin (-nen) | actress |
| der Komiker (-) <br> die Komikerin (-nen) | comedian (m/f) |
| berühmt | famous |
| die Bühne (-n) | stage |
| Karten reservieren | to book tickets |
| die Vorverkaufsstelle (-n) | booking office |
| ausverkauft | sold out |

| | |
|---|---|
| der Anfang (¨e) | beginning |
| anfangen (er fängt ... an) (s; sep) <br> beginnen (er beginnt) (s; insep) | to begin |
| das Ende | end |
| die Aufführung (-en) <br> die Vorstellung (-en) | performance |
| die Vorstellung ist um halb elf zu Ende | the performance finishes at 10.30 |
| die Inszenierung (-en) | production |
| die Komödie (-n) | comedy |
| die Tragödie (-n) | tragedy |
| das Ballett (-e) | ballet |
| die Oper (-n) | opera |
| die Garderobe (-n) | cloakroom |

## n Essen gehen     Eating out

| | |
|---|---|
| ins Restaurant gehen* (s) | to go to a restaurant |
| der Imbiß (Imbisse) | snack |
| zum Mitnehmen | take-away |
| der Würstchenstand (¨e) | sausage/hot-dog stand |
| die Imbißstube (-n) | snack bar |
| das Restaurant (-s) | restaurant |

| | |
|---|---|
| **der Kellner (-)** | waiter |
| **die Kellnerin (-nen)** | waitress |
| **Herr Ober!** | waiter! |
| **Fräulein!** | waitress! |

| | |
|---|---|
| **das Menü (-s)** | set meal |
| **die Speisekarte (-n)** | menu |
| **die Tageskarte (-n)** | menu of the day |
| **die Getränkekarte/Weinkarte (-n)** | drinks menu, wine list |
| **bestellen** (*insep*) | to order |
| **die Bestellung (-en)** | order |
| **servieren** } | to serve |
| **bedienen** (*insep*) } | |
| **die Vorspeise (-n)** | starter |
| **das Hauptgericht (-e)** | main course |
| **der Nachtisch (-e)** | dessert |
| **die Portion (-en)** | helping |
| **der Kinderteller (-)** | children's portion |
| **probieren** | to try out, taste |
| **schlucken** | to swallow |
| **reichen** | to pass |

| | |
|---|---|
| **zahlen, bitte!** | the bill, please! |
| **zusammen** | together |
| **getrennt** | separately |
| **trennen** | to separate |
| **das stimmt so** | keep the change |

 See also Food, page 36.

## 4 *Meinungen* *Opinions*

### a Allgemeines General

| | |
|---|---|
| **die Behauptung (-en)** | statement |
| **die Meinung (-en)** | opinion |
| **denken (er denkt)** (*irreg w*) | to think |
| **glauben** | to believe, think |
| **sich** (*Dat*) **vorstellen** (*sep*) | to imagine |
| **ich kenne mich da nicht aus** | I don't know much about that |
| **sicher sein** | to be certain |
| **recht haben** | to be right |
| **unrecht haben** | to be wrong |

### b Fragen stellen

### Inquiring

| | |
|---|---|
| wie findest du...? | |
| was hältst du von...? | what do you think about...? |
| was denkst du über...? | |
| was meinst du dazu? | what do you think about that? |
| wie gefällt dir...? | how do you like...? |

### c Mögen

### Likes

| | |
|---|---|
| gefallen (+*Dat*) (es gefällt) (*s*) | to please, appeal to |
| das gefällt mir sehr | I like that a lot |
| diese gefallen ihr sehr | she likes these a lot |
| er freute sich ebenso wie ich | he was just as pleased as I was |

| | |
|---|---|
| zufrieden mit (+*Dat*) | satisfied with |
| ich bin damit zufrieden | I'm quite happy with it |

| | |
|---|---|
| ziemlich gut | fairly good |
| ganz gut | pretty good |
| total gut | really good |
| prima | |
| klasse | great |
| spitze | |
| ausgezeichnet | |
| großartig | tremendous |
| fabelhaft | splendid |
| toll | fantastic |
| wunderbar | wonderful |
| super | super |
| echt super (*colloquial*) | really super |
| am liebsten | best of all |
| Mensch! | wow! |
| unvergeßlich | unforgettable |
| lustig | funny |
| amüsant | amusing |
| überraschend | suprising |
| erstaunlich | astonishing |
| erstaunt | astonished |
| ich bin dafür | |
| ich bin damit einverstanden | I agree with it |

## d Gleichgültigkeit

| | |
|---|---|
| es geht | it's OK |
| das ist mir gleich/egal | it's all the same to me |
| das ist mir Wurst (*colloquial*) | I don't care |
| es kommt darauf an | it depends |
| das interessiert mich nicht ⎱<br>ich interessiere mich nicht dafür ⎰ | that doesn't interest me |
| das sagt mir nichts | that means nothing to me |
| es macht nichts | it doesn't matter |

## Indifference

## e Nicht mögen

| | |
|---|---|
| ich halte nichts davon | I don't like it |
| ich bin dagegen | I am against it |
| das ärgert mich | that annoys me |
| ich kann das nicht leiden | I can't stand it |
| ich finde es ⎰ langweilig<br> ⎱ (zu) dumm | I think it's ⎰ boring<br> ⎱ (really) stupid, silly |
| das ist doch Blödsinn | that's stupid |
| das ist schlimm | that's bad/serious |
| schrecklich ⎱<br>furchtbar ⎰ | horrible, awful |
| nutzlos | useless |
| enttäuschend | disappointing |
| unangenehm | unpleasant |
| ekelhaft | disgusting |
| mies | rotten, lousy |
| ärgerlich | annoying |
| beunruhigend | worrying |
| peinlich | embarrassing |
| komisch | odd |

## Dislikes

## 5 Besondere Gelegenheiten

## Special occasions

## a Jährliche Feste

| | |
|---|---|
| (der/das) Silvester | New Year's Eve |
| (das) Neujahr | New Year's Day |
| der Valentinstag | St Valentine's Day |
| (der) Fastnachtsdienstag | Shrove Tuesday |
| der Fasching (-e *or* -s) | Shrovetide carnival |

## Annual festivals

| | |
|---|---|
| (der) Aschermittwoch | Ash Wednesday |
| (der) Karfreitag | Good Friday |
| (das) Ostern | Easter |
| der Maifeiertag | May Day |
| (die) Christi Himmelfahrt | Ascension |
| (das) Pfingsten | Whitsun |
| der Vatertag | Fathers' Day |
| der Muttertag | Mothers' Day |
| (das) Allerheiligen | All Saints' Day |
| (das) Weihnachten | Christmas |
| der Heilige Abend | Christmas Eve |
| der erste Weihnachtstag | Christmas Day |
| der zweite Weihnachtstag | Boxing Day |
| der Weihmachtsmann | Father Christmas |
| Sankt Nikolaus | Santa Claus (St Nicholas) |
| Knecht Ruprecht | (assistant to St Nikolaus) |

| | |
|---|---|
| zu Weihnachten/Ostern | at Christmas/Easter |
| zum Neujahr | at New Year |
| frohes neues Jahr! | Happy New Year |
| fröhliche Ostern! | Happy Easter |
| frohe Weihnachten! | Happy Christmas |
| das Weihnachtslied | Christmas carol |
| die Bescherung | giving out of Christmas presents |
| in die Kirche gehen | to go to church |
| zur Messe gehen | to go to Mass |
| religiös | religious |

| | |
|---|---|
| das Passah | Passover |
| der Ramadan | Ramadan |

## Jetzt bist du dran! 31

*Wie heißen diese besonderen Tage?*

What are these special days called?

 1
 2
 3
 4
 5

| b Familienfeste | Family festivals |
|---|---|
| die Geburt (-en) | birth |
| der Geburtstag (-e) | birthday |
| herzlichen Glückwunsch zum Geburtstag! | Happy birthday |
| der Namenstag (-e) | name day, Saint's day |
| die Geburtstagsparty (-s) | birthday party |
| einladen (er lädt ... ein) (s; sep) | to invite |
| die Einladung (-en) | invitation |
| annehmen (er nimmt ... an) (s; sep) | to accept |
| eine Einladung ablehnen (sep) | to decline an invitation |
| feiern | to celebrate |
| gratulieren (+Dat) | to congratulate |
| die Glückwünsche (pl) | congratulations |
| schenken | to give |
| das Geschenk (-e) | present |
| erhalten (er erhält) (s; insep) bekommen (er bekommt) (s; insep) | to receive |
| die Freude | delight, joy |
| sich freuen über (+Acc) | to be glad (at/about) |
| überraschen (insep) | to surprise |
| die Überraschung (-en) | surprise |
| die Verwandten (pl; adj. noun) | relations |

| | |
|---|---|
| die Bekannten (*pl; adj. noun*) | friends/acquaintances |
| die Hochzeit (-en) | wedding |
| die Braut | bride |
| der Bräutigam | bridegroom |
| die Silberhochzeit | Silver Wedding |
| die Konfirmation | confirmation |
| die Erstkommunion | first Communion |
| der Sabbat (-e) | Sabbath |
| das Bar Mizwa | bar mitzvah |

 See May I introduce myself? pages 53–4.

## 6 *Urlaub* Holidays

### a Allgemeines     General

| | |
|---|---|
| die Ferien (*pl*) | holidays (*time off school*) |
| die Schulferien (*pl*) | school holidays |
| die Weihnachtsferien (*pl*) | Christmas holidays |
| die Osterferien (*pl*) | Easter holidays |
| die Sommerferien (*pl*) | summer holidays |
| die Ferien in der Mitte des Trimesters | half-term holidays (Great Britain) |
| frei haben | to have time off |
| der Urlaub (-e) | holiday (*going away*) |
| der Familienurlaub | family holiday |
| in Urlaub gehen* (*s*) | to go away on holiday |
| im Urlaub sein* (*s*) | to be away on holiday |
| wegfahren* (er fährt ... weg) (*s; sep*) | to go away |
| ins Ausland fahren* (er fährt) (*s*) | to go abroad |
| im Ausland sein* (*s*) | to be abroad |
| fremd | unfamiliar |

| | |
|---|---|
| organisieren | to organise |
| packen | to pack |
| auspacken | to unpack |
| verbringen (er verbringt) (*irreg w; insep*) | to spend (*time*) |
| die Erholung | relaxation, rest |
| (sich) ausruhen (*sep*) | to have a rest |
| braun werden* (*s*) | to get a tan |

| | |
|---|---|
| **erleben** (*insep*) | to experience |
| **Neues erleben** | to see something new |
| **kennenlernen** (*sep*) | to get to know |
| **besuchen** (*insep*) | to visit (*person*) |
| **besichtigen** (*insep*) | to visit (*place*), have a look round |

| | |
|---|---|
| **die Postkarte** (-n) | postcard |
| **die Ansichtskarte** (-n) | picture postcard |
| **das Andenken/Reiseandenken** (-) ⎫ | |
| **das Souvenir** (-s) ⎭ | souvenir |
| **der Schlüsselring** (-e) | key-ring |
| **das Geschenk** (-e) | present |
| **das Kölnisch Wasser** | eau de Cologne |

| | |
|---|---|
| **der Ferienjob** (-s) | holiday job |
| **Arbeit finden** (er findet) (s) | to get work |
| **verdienen** (*insep*) | to earn |

## b Unterkunft — Accommodation

| | |
|---|---|
| **der Zimmernachweis** (-e) | tourist accommodation agency |
| **die Unterkunft** | accommodation |
| **das Hotel** (-s) | hotel |
| **das Drei-Sterne-Hotel** (-s) | 3-star hotel |
| **der Komfort** | luxury, comfort |
| **das Hotel garni** (*both words add -s*) | bed and breakfast hotel |
| **die Pension** (-en) ⎫ | |
| **das Fremdenheim** (-e) ⎭ | guest house |
| **Fremdenzimmer** | Bed & Breakfast |
| **das Gasthaus** (¨er) ⎫ | |
| **der Gasthof** (¨e) ⎭ | inn |
| **das Rasthaus** (¨er) ⎫ | |
| **der Rasthof** (¨e) ⎭ | inn on motorway |
| **das Motel** (-s) | motel |

| | |
|---|---|
| **übernachten** (*insep*) | to spend the night |
| **die Übernachtung** (-en) | overnight stay |
| **der Aufenthalt** | stay |
| **in einem Hotel wohnen** | to stay in a hotel |
| **bleiben*** (er bleibt) (s) | to remain, stay |
| **die Vollpension** | full board |
| **die Halbpension** | half board |
| **die Bedienung** | service |

| | |
|---|---|
| einschließlich Frühstück <br> Frühstück inbegriffen } | breakfast included |
| inklusive <br> einschl. (einschließlich) } | included |
| das Mittagessen | lunch |
| das Abendessen | evening meal |
| warme Küche | hot meals |

| | |
|---|---|
| der Direktor (-en) | manager |
| die Leitung | management |
| der Wirt/Gastwirt (-e) | landlord (*of pub/restaurant*) |
| die Wirtin/Gastwirtin (-nen) | landlady (*of pub/restaurant*) |
| der Empfang <br> die Rezeption } | reception |
| die Anmeldung | |
| der Empfangschef (-s) | receptionist (*m*) |
| die Empfangsdame (-n) | receptionist (*f*) |
| sich anmelden (*sep*) | to register |
| das Formular (-e) | form |
| das Anmeldeformular (-e) | registration form |
| ausfüllen (*sep*) | to fill in |
| das Hotelverzeichnis | hotel register |
| die Unterschrift (-en) | signature |
| unterschreiben <br> (er unterschreibt) (*s; insep*) | to sign |
| reservieren | to book |
| wir haben noch ein Zimmer frei | we still have one room free |
| das Hotel ist voll belegt | the hotel is full |
| ab wann? | from when? |
| bis wann? | until when? |
| die Ankunft | arrival |
| die Abreise | departure |
| die Nacht (¨e) | night |
| pro Nacht | per night |
| die Rechnung (-en) | bill |
| die Rechnung fertigmachen (*sep*) | to prepare the bill |
| kosten | to cost |
| die Kosten (*pl*) | costs, expenses |
| der Preis (-e) | price |
| die Mehrwertsteuer (MWSt) | value added tax (VAT) |
| inklusive Mehrwertsteuer | VAT included |
| der Scheck/Reisescheck (-s) | (traveller's) cheque |

| | |
|---|---|
| sich beklagen (über+*Acc*) (*insep*) | |
| sich beschweren (über+*Acc*) (*insep*) | to complain (about) |
| die Beschwerde (-n) | complaint |
| | |
| das Hotelzimmer (-) | hotel room |
| das Einzelzimmer (-) | |
| Einbettzimmer (-) | single room |
| das Zweibettzimmer (-) | twin bedded room |
| das Doppelzimmer (-) | double room |
| der Stock (Stockwerke) | storey, floor |
| einfach | simple |
| ruhig | peaceful, quiet |
| der Balkon (-s) | balcony |
| die Aussicht (-en) | |
| der Blick (-e) | view |
| nach vorne/nach hinten | at the front/back |
| mit Blick auf die Berge | with a view of the mountains |
| mit Dusche/Bad usw | with shower/bath etc |
| mit Waschgelegenheit | with washing facilities |
| mit fließendem/heißem Wasser | with running/hot water |
| eine eigene Toilette | a toilet of one's own |
| der Schlüssel (-) | key |
| | |
| der Koffer (-) | suitcase |
| die Reisetasche (-n) | travel-bag |
| das Gepäck | luggage |
| auspacken (*sep*) | to unpack |
| der Portier (-s) | porter |
| der Aufzug (¨e) | |
| der Fahrstuhl (¨e) | lift |
| der Lift (-e *or* -s) | |
| | |
| der Speisesaal (-säle) | dining room |
| die Bar (-s) | bar |
| die Theke (-n) | bar (*counter*) |
| der Feuerlöscher (-) | fire extinguisher |
| parken | to park |
| der Parkplatz (¨e) | car park |
| die Tiefgarage (-n) | underground car park |

See also Bedroom vocabulary, pages 73–4.

## c Die Ferienwohnung (-en) — Holiday flat

| | |
|---|---|
| mieten | to rent (*from someone*) |
| vermieten (*insep*) | to rent (*to someone*) |
| der Vermieter (-) | landlord |
| die Vermieterin (-nen) | landlady |
| der Mieter (-) | tenant |
| preiswert | inexpensive |
| bequem | convenient |
| praktisch | practical |
| die Selbstversorgung | self-catering |
| saubermachen (*sep*) | to do the cleaning |

 See also At home, pages 66–8.

## d Die Jugendherberge — The youth hostel

| | |
|---|---|
| die Jugendherberge (-n) | youth hostel |
| DJH = Deutsche Jugendherbergen | (*German YHA*) |
| der Herbergsvater (¨) | warden (*m*) |
| die Herbergsmutter (¨) | warden (*f*)/warden's wife |
| die Herbergseltern (*pl*) | wardens |
| der Gast (¨e) | guest (*m/f*) |
| das Mitglied (-er) | member |
| der Ausweis (-e) | membership card |
| die Unterkunft | accommodation |
| unterkommen* (er kommt unter) (*s; sep*) | to find accommodation |
| der Schlafraum (¨e) | dormitory |
| buchen | to book |
| das Schwarze Brett | notice board |
| im voraus | in advance |
| erlauben (*insep*) | to allow |
| verbieten (er verbietet) (*s; insep*) | to forbid |
| erlaubt | allowed |
| verboten | forbidden |
| (nicht) gestattet | (not) allowed |
| leihen (er leiht) (*s*) | to lend, loan, borrow, hire |
| borgen | to borrow |
| der Schlafsack (¨e) | sleeping-bag |
| der Rucksack (¨e) | rucksack |
| wandern* | to hike |
| die Wanderung (-en) | hike |

## e Zelten — Camping

| | |
|---|---|
| das Camping | camping |
| zum Camping fahren* (s) | to go camping |
| zelten | to camp |
| der Campingplatz (¨e) }<br>der Zeltplatz (¨e) } | campsite |
| das Zelt (-e) | tent |
| ein Zelt aufschlagen }<br>(er schlägt ... auf) (s; sep) }<br>ein Zelt aufbauen (sep) } | to put up a tent |
| ein Zelt abbauen (sep) | to take down a tent |
| der Schatten (-) | shade, shadow |
| der Wohnwagen (-) | caravan |

| | |
|---|---|
| das Büro (-s) | office |
| die Gebühr (-en) | fee |
| die Quittung (-en) | receipt |
| die Platzruhe }<br>die Nachtruhe } | time for silence at night |
| der Kiosk (-e) | kiosk |
| der Laden (¨) | shop |
| der Spielplatz (¨e) | playground |
| der Waschraum (¨e) | washroom |
| die Spülküche (-n) | washing-up room |
| das Trinkwasser | drinking water |

| | |
|---|---|
| der Campingartikel (-) | item of camping equipment |
| tragbar | portable |
| zusammenklappbar | folding |
| der Klappstuhl (¨e) | folding chair |
| der Klapptisch (-e) | folding table |
| die Batterie (-n) | battery |
| der Strom | electric current/electricity |
| die Elektrizität | electricity |
| anschließen (er schließt an) (s; sep) | to plug in |
| das Feuer | fire |
| das Campinggas | camping gas |
| der Campingkocher (-) | camping stove |
| die Campingliege (-n) | camp bed |
| die Luftmatratze (-n) | air bed |
| die Luftpumpe (-n) | air pump |
| aufpumpen (sep) | to pump up |

 See also In the kitchen, pages 70–2 for list of equipment.

# Jetzt bist du dran! 32

Finde die zwei Hälften der Sätze, die zueinander passen!

Find the two halves of the sentences that go together.

| | |
|---|---|
| Wir packten die Koffer | nicht vergessen! |
| Das Luftkissenfahrzeug fährt | oft voll belegt. |
| Wir dürfen den Fotoapparat | in Straßburg zu übernachten. |
| Wir haben die Schiffskarten | kein sehr teures Hotel. |
| Wir wollen durch den Tunnel | war leider außer Betrieb. |
| Man muß eine gute Stunde | vor der Landung zu haben. |
| Du brauchst ja keine Angst | alle ins Auto. |
| Wir haben vor, unterwegs | um unsere Ausweise. |
| Wir suchen | nach Brüssel fahren. |
| Der Herbergsvater bat | schon im voraus gekauft. |
| Die Campingplätze sind im Juli | vor der Abfahrtszeit da sein. |
| Der Fahrstuhl im Hotel | schon um 10.30 Uhr ab. |

 # Jetzt bist du dran! 33

Welche Wörter gehören zusammen?

Which pair of words belong together?

| | |
|---|---|
| die Bar | die Aussicht |
| die Kellnerin | die Empfangsdame |
| der Aufzug | der Koffer |
| das Zimmer | die Abreise |
| der Parkplatz | der Schnaps |
| der Balkon | die Unterschrift |
| die Anmeldung | die Bedienung |
| der Gepäckträger | die Übernachtung |
| die Rechnung | außer Betrieb |
| das Formular | die Tiefgarage |
| der Schlafraum | die Spülküche |
| die Batterie | der Stuhl |
| die Dusche | der Ausweis |
| die Platzruhe | zahlen |
| klappbar | der Rucksack |
| das Zelt | Mitternacht |
| das Geschirr | der Waschraum |
| die Gebühr | der Schlafsack |
| wandern | die Taschenlampe |
| das Mitglied | aufschlagen |

## f Schüleraustausch — School exchanges

| | |
|---|---|
| der Austausch | exchange |
| die Klassenfahrt (-en) | class trip |
| der Ausflug (-̈e) | excursion |
| besuchen (*insep*) | to visit |
| die Sitte (-n) | custom |
| ausländisch | foreign |
| das Heimweh | home-sickness |
| müde | tired |
| danken (+*Dat*) | to thank |
| dankbar | grateful |
| sich bedanken (*insep*) | to thank (*formal*) |
| herzlich | hearty/heartily |

## g Am Meer — At the seaside

| | |
|---|---|
| das Meer (-e) ⎫ die See ⎬ | sea |
| der Strand (-̈e) | beach |
| die Küste (-n) | coast |
| der Badeort (-e) | (seaside) resort |
| der Stein (-e) | stone |
| der Felsen (-) | rock |
| die Klippe (-n) | cliff |
| der Sand | sand |
| die Welle (-n) | wave |
| sauber | clean |
| schmutzig | dirty |
| baden | to bathe |
| schwimmen* (er schwimmt) (*s*) | to swim |
| der Badeanzug (-̈e) | swimsuit |
| die Badehose (-n) | swimming trunks |
| der Bikini (-s) | bikini |
| das Badezeug | swimming gear |
| der Schnorchel (-) | snorkel |
| schnorcheln gehen* (*s*) | to go snorkling |
| das Surfboard (-s) ⎫ das Surfbrett (-er) ⎬ | surfboard |
| surfen | to go surfing |
| die Sandburg (-en) | sand castle |
| der Liegestuhl (-̈e) | deckchair |
| der Strandkorb (-̈e) | wicker beach-chair with hood (*German*) |

| | |
|---|---|
| **sich hinlegen (sep)** | to lie down |
| **liegen (er liegt) (s)** | to be lying down |
| **die Luftmatratze (-n)** | air-bed |
| **sich sonnen** ⎫<br>**in der Sonne liegen (s)** ⎬ | to sunbathe |
| **braun werden\* (s)** | to get a tan |
| **das Sonnenöl** | suntan oil |
| **die Sonnencreme** ⎫<br>**die Sonnenmilch** ⎬ | suncream |
| **einreiben (er reibt ... ein)**<br>**(s; sep)** | to rub in |
| **(der) Sonnenbrand** | sunburn |
| **die Sonnenbrille (-n)** | pair of sunglasses |

 See also Sport, pages 84–7.

## Jetzt bist du dran! 34

*Was sind diese Sachen?*     *What are these things?*

1  2  3  4  5

## h Der Wintersport

## Winter sports

| | |
|---|---|
| **ins Gebirge fahren\*** | to go to the mountains |
| **im Gebirge wohnen** | to stay in the mountains |
| **der Skiort (-e)** | ski resort |

| | |
|---|---|
| die Ausrüstung mieten | to hire the equipment |
| skilaufen* (er läuft ... Ski) | to ski |
| skifahren* (er fährt ... Ski) | |
| Skilaufen/Skifahren | skiing |
| der Langlauf | cross-country skiing |
| der Ski (-er or -) | ski |
| der Skistock (¨e) | ski stick |
| die Skipiste (-n) | ski-run |
| der Skilift (-e or -s) | ski-lift |
| die Seilbahn (-en) | cable-car |
| gefährlich | dangerous |
| die Lawine (-n) | avalanche |
| die Eisbahn (-en) | ice-skating rink |
| Schlittschuhlaufen | ice-skating |
| Schlittschuh laufen* (er läuft) | to go ice-skating |
| eislaufen* (s; sep) | |

# C:The world around us

## 1 Die Stadt — The town/city

### a Die Beschreibung — Description

| | |
|---|---|
| die Stadt (¨e) | town, city |
| die Hauptstadt (¨e) | capital city |
| das Dorf (¨er) | village |
| die Ortschaft (-en) | village, town |
| der Ort (-e) | place |
| der Stadtteil (-e) } das Viertel (-) | district, part of town |
| der Kreis (-e) | district |
| die Kreisstadt (¨e) | chief town of a district |
| der Vorort (-e) | suburb |
| der Bezirk (-e) | district, area |
| das Gebiet (-e) | area |
| das Wohngebiet (-e) | residential area |
| das Industriegebiet (-e) | industrial area |
| der Einwohner (-) | inhabitant |
| die Altstadt | old part of town |
| historisch | historic |
| das Fachwerk | half-timbering |
| die Innenstadt | centre of town |
| die Stadtmitte/die City } das Stadtzentrum | town/city centre |
| von ... umgeben | surrounded by... |
| der Platz (¨e) | square |
| der Bürgersteig (-e) | pavement |
| die Passage (-n) | arcade |
| der Fluß (Flüsse) | river |
| das Rathaus (¨er) | town hall |
| die Polizei | police |
| die Polizeiwache | police station |
| die Feuerwache (-n) | fire station |
| die Feuerwehr | fire brigade |
| das Gebäude (-) | building |
| das Bürogebäude (-) | office-block |
| die Baustelle (-n) | building-site |
| die Kirche (-n) | church |

| | |
|---|---|
| der Dom (-e) <br> das Münster (-) } | cathedral |
| die Kathedrale (-n) | cathedral (*outside Germany*) |
| der Gottesdienst (-e) | church service |
| die Messe (-n) | Mass |
| der Friedhof (̈-e) | cemetery |
| | |
| die Einkaufsstraße (-n) | shopping-street |
| das Einkaufszentrum (-zentren) | shopping-centre |
| das Warenhaus (̈-er) <br> das Kaufhaus (̈-er) } | department store |
| das Geschäft (-e) | shop, business |
| der Laden (̈-) | shop |
| die Boutique (-n) | boutique |
| der Marktplatz (̈-e) | market place |
| der Markt (̈-e) | market |
| der Stand (̈-e) | stall |
| das Café (-s) | tea-shop |
| die Bierhalle (-n) | beer-hall |
| die Fabrik (-en) | factory |
| | |
| der Bahnhof (̈-e) | railway station |
| der Busbahnhof (̈-e) | bus station |
| die U-Bahnstation (-en) | underground station |
| der Parkplatz (̈-e) | car-park |
| das Parkhaus (̈-er) <br> die Hochgarage (-n) } | multi-storey car-park |
| die Tiefgarage (-n) | underground car-park |
| die Tankstelle (-n) | petrol station |
| | |
| das Schloß (Schlösser) | castle, stately home |
| die Burg (-en) | castle, fortress |
| die Stadtmauer (-n) | city wall |
| das Denkmal (̈-er) | monument, memorial |
| die Säule (-n) | column |
| der Turm (̈-e) | tower |
| der Kirchturm (̈-e) | church tower, steeple |
| die Bibliothek (-en) <br> die Bücherei (-en) } | library |
| das Museum (Museen) | museum |
| die Galerie/Kunstgalerie (-n) | art gallery |
| das Theater (-) | theatre |
| die Oper (-n) | opera |
| das Opernhaus (̈-er) | opera house |

| | |
|---|---|
| **das Kino (-s)** | cinema |
| **die Diskothek (-en)** } | |
| **die Disco/Disko (-s)** } | disco |
| **das Schwimmbad (¨er)** | swimming pool |
| **die Eisbahn (-en)** | ice rink |
| **das Stadion (Stadien)** | stadium |

 See also Travel and transport, pages 142–55.

## b Im Verkehrsamt    At the tourist office

| | |
|---|---|
| **das Verkehrsbüro (-s)** } | |
| **das Verkehrsamt (¨er)** } | tourist office |
| **sich erkundigen** | to ask for information |
| **die Auskunft (¨e)** | (piece of) information |
| **was gibt es hier zu sehen?** | what is there to see here? |
| **die Sehenswürdigkeiten (*pl*)** | sights |
| **sehenswert** | worth seeing |
| **besichtigen (*insep*)** | to visit, have a look round |
| **besuchen (*insep*)** | to visit |
| **der Besucher (-)** | visitor |
| **der Tourist (-en, -en)** | tourist (*m*) |
| **die Touristin (-nen)** | tourist (*f*) |
| **bummeln** | to stroll |
| **der Stadtbummel (-)** | stroll through town |
| **die Umgebung (-en)** | surroundings |
| **empfehlen (er empfiehlt) (*s*)** | to recommend |
| **das Plakat (-e)** | poster |
| **die Broschüre (-n)** | brochure |
| **der Prospekt (-e)** | brochure, pamphlet |
| **der Stadtplan (¨e)** | street-map |
| **die Rundfahrt (-en)** | tour (*by bus etc*) |
| **der Rundgang (¨e)** | tour (*on foot*) |
| **eine Rundfahrt machen** | to go on a tour |
| **die Führung (-en) (durch...)** | guided tour (of...) |
| **führen** | to lead |
| **der Reiseführer (-)** | guidebook |
| **der Reiseleiter (-)** | guide, courier |
| **der Ausflug (¨e)** | excursion |
| **eine Fahrt ins Blaue** | a mystery tour |
| **stattfinden (es findet statt)** | |
| **(*s; sep*)** | to take place |
| **der Eintritt** | entrance, admission fee |
| **die Gebühr (-en)** | fee, charge |

| | |
|---|---|
| **kostenlos** | free, for nothing |
| **der Erwachsene** (*adj. noun*) | adult |
| **die Ermäßigung** (-en) | reduction |
| **die Schülerermäßigung** (-en) | reduction for people at school |
| **die Gruppe** (-n) | group |

---

 ## Jetzt bist du dran! 35

*Was befindet sich wo? Finde die richtigen Wörter für die Bilder, und schreib Sätze darüber!*

What goes where? Match up the words with the pictures and write sentences.

**Beispiel:** a = 8 Der Brunnen befindet sich im Park.

(1) *das Verkehrsamt*

(3) der Markt

(2) die Fabrik

(6) **die Kunstgalerie**

(9) der Zoo

(8) **der Park**

(5) der Friedhof

(7) **die Polizeiwache**

(4) die Bibliothek

---

### c Richtungen

### Directions

| | |
|---|---|
| **der Stadtplan** (-̈e) | street-map |
| **sich erkundigen** (*insep*) | to ask for information |
| **wie komme ich zum Markt?** | how do I get to the market? |

| | |
|---|---|
| **abbiegen\* (er biegt ... ab)** | |
| **(s; sep)** | to turn |
| **gesperrt** | closed, blocked |
| **vor** | in front of |
| **hinter** | behind |
| **neben** | next to |
| **gegenüber** | opposite |
| **links** | on the left |
| **rechts** | on the right |
| **auf der linken/rechten Seite** | on the left/right |
| **nach links/rechts** | to the left/right |
| **gleich hier** | immediately here |
| **drüben** | over there |
| **(immer) geradeaus** | (keep going) straight on |
| **die erste (Straße) links** | first on the left |
| **genau 100 Meter** | exactly 100 metres |
| **nächst-** | next |
| **die nächste Straße rechts** | the next street on the right |
| **in der Nähe von (+Dat)** | near |
| **fern** | distant |
| **(nicht) weit von (+Dat)** | (not) far from |
| **unweit von (+Dat)** | not far from |
| **anderthalb Kilometer entfernt** | 1½ km away |
| **der Kilometer (-) (km)** | kilometre |
| **die Meile (-n)** | mile |
| **es gibt (+Acc)** | there is, there are |
| **es gibt einen Baum an der Ecke** | there is a tree on the corner |
| **sich befinden (er befindet sich)** | |
| **(s; insep)** | to be (*in a certain place*) |
| **liegen (er liegt) (s)** | |
| **überall** | everywhere |
| **irgendwo** | somewhere or other |
| **zeigen** | to show, point |
| **folgen\* (+Dat)** | to follow |
| **überqueren (insep)** | to cross |
| **sich verirren (insep)** | to get lost |
| **sich verlaufen (er verläuft sich)** | |
| **(s; insep)** | to get lost (*walking*) |
| **sich verfahren (er verfährt sich)** | |
| **(s; insep)** | to get lost (*driving*) |

| die Autobahn (-en) | motorway |
| die Straße (-n) (Str.) | street, road |
| die Schnellstraße (-n) | dual carriageway |
| die Hauptstraße (-n) | main road, high street |
| die Querstraße (-n) die Nebenstraße (-n) } | side street |
| die Gasse (-n) | small street, lane |
| die Einbahnstraße (-n) | one-way street |
| die Ringstraße (-n) | ring-road |
| die Sackgasse (-n) | cul-de-sac |
| die Fußgängerzone (-n) | pedestrian precinct |
| der Zebrastreifen (-) | zebra crossing |
| der Bahnübergang (¨e) | level crossing |
| die Kurve (-n) | bend |
| die Ecke (-n) | corner |
| die Kreuzung (-en) | crossroads |
| die Ampel (-n) | traffic-lights |
| die Bushaltestelle (-n) | bus stop |
| die Straßenbahnhaltestelle (-n) | tram stop |
| die Brücke (-n) | bridge |
| die Überführung (-en) | flyover, footbridge |
| die Unterführung (-en) | subway |
| der Tunnel (-) | tunnel |
| die Umleitung (-en) | diversion |
| die Straßenarbeiten (*pl*) | roadworks |

## Jetzt bist du dran! 36

| Welche Wörter gehören zusammen? | Which words belong together? |
|---|---|

| | |
|---|---|
| die Brücke | das Verkehrsbüro |
| die Ampel | die Kirche |
| eine Turnhalle | der Bahnhof |
| der Bahnsteig | der neue Stadtteil |
| die Broschüre | der Fluß |
| die Verkäuferin | der Markt |
| der Turm | das Sportzentrum |
| das Hochhaus | die Kreuzung |
| Obst | das Warenhaus |

# Jetzt bist du dran! 37

Finde die richtigen Wörter für die Bilder, und ergänze die Sätze mit ,zum' oder ,zur'!

Match up the words with the pictures and complete the sentences using 'zum' or 'zur'.

**Beispiel:** *Wie komme ich* zum Bahnhof?

1 *Wie komme ich* .............................................. ?

2 *Wie komme ich* .............................................. ?

3 *Wie komme ich* .............................................. ?

4 *Wie komme ich* .............................................. ?

5 *Wie komme ich* .............................................. ?

6 *Wie komme ich* .............................................. ?

7 *Wie komme ich* .............................................. ?

8 *Wie komme ich* .............................................. ?

9 *Wie komme ich* .............................................. ?

## 2 Die Natur Nature

### a Die Landschaft Scenery

| | |
|---|---|
| die Natur | nature |
| aufs Land fahren* (er fährt) (s) | to go into the country |
| auf dem Land(e) sein* | to be in the country |
| die Gegend (-en) | area, region |
| das Dorf (¨er) | village |
| die Landschaft (-en) | scenery, landscape |
| die frische Luft | fresh air |
| still | quiet, silent |
| ruhig | peaceful, quiet |
| eine ruhige Stelle | a quiet spot |

| | |
|---|---|
| der Baum (¨e) | tree |
| das Blatt (¨er) | leaf |
| das Nest (-er) | nest |
| der Obstgarten (¨) | orchard |
| die Obstplantage (-n) | orchard (*commercial*) |
| der Obstbaum (¨e) | fruit tree |
| der Apfelbaum (¨e) | apple tree |
| der Birnbaum (¨e) | pear tree |
| die Eiche (-n) | oak |
| die Eichel (-n) | acorn |
| die Buche (-n) | beech |
| die Birke (-n) | birch |
| die Tanne (-n) ⎫ der Tannenbaum (¨e) ⎬ | fir tree |
| der Tannenzapfen (-) | fir cone |
| die Weide (-n) | willow |

| | |
|---|---|
| der Wald (¨er) | wood, forest |
| der Forst (-e) | commercially cultivated forest |
| der Dschungel (-) | jungle |
| die Erde (-n) | earth |
| das Feld (-er) | field (*for crops*) |
| die Wiese (-n) | meadow, field (*for animals*) |
| das Gras | grass |
| grasen | to graze |
| die Hecke (-n) | hedge |
| der Weg (-e) | path |
| der Fußweg (-e) | footpath |

| | |
|---|---|
| der Wegweiser (-) | signpost |
| der Zaun (¨e) | fence |
| der Fluß (Flüsse) | river |
| das Ufer (-) | river-bank |
| der Bach (¨e) | stream |
| fließen* (er fließt) (s) | to flow |
| die Brücke (-n) | bridge |
| der See (-n) | lake |
| die Insel (-n) | island |
| der Teich (-e) | pond |
| der Berg (-e) | mountain, large hill |
| das Gebirge (-) | range of mountains |
| der Gipfel (-) | summit, peak |
| der Hügel (-) | hill (*small*) |
| das Tal (¨er) | valley |
| die Talsperre (-n) | dam |
| tief | deep |
| hoch | high |
| *but* hoh- *with an ending as* | |
| *adjective*: ein hoher Berg | a high mountain |
| steil | steep |
| flach | flat, shallow |

| | |
|---|---|
| der Bauer (-n, -n) | farmer |
| der Bauernhof (¨e) | farm |
| das Bauernhaus (¨er) | farmhouse |
| die Scheune (-n) | barn |
| der Stall (¨e) | stable |
| der Kuhstall (¨e) | cowshed |
| der Schweinestall (¨e) | pigsty |
| die Mühle (-n) | mill |
| die Windmühle (-n) | windmill |
| das Getreide | corn |
| das Stroh | straw |
| das Heu | hay |
| anbauen (*sep*) | to grow (*something*) |
| die Ernte (-n) | harvest(ing) |

## b Tiere, Vögel und Insekten    Animals, birds and insects

| | |
|---|---|
| das Tier (-e) | animal |
| füttern | to feed |
| das Vieh | cattle, livestock |
| die Kuh (¨e) | cow |

| | |
|---|---|
| der Stier (-e) | bull |
| das Kalb (¨er) | calf |
| muhen | to moo, to low |
| das Pferd (-e) | horse |
| die Stute (-n) | mare |
| das Pony (-s) | pony |
| der Esel (-) | donkey |
| das Schwein (-e) | pig |
| das Ferkel (-) | piglet |
| das Schaf (-e) | sheep |
| das Lamm (¨er) | lamb |
| mähen | to bleat, to baa |
| die Ziege (-n) | goat |
| der Vogel (¨) | bird |
| das Huhn (¨er) | chicken |
| der Hahn (¨e) | cock |
| die Henne (-n) | hen |
| das Ei (-er) | egg |
| krähen | to crow |
| die Ente (-n) | duck |
| die Gans (¨e) | goose |
| das Kaninchen (-) | rabbit |
| der Hase (-n, -n) | hare |
| das Eichhörnchen (-) | squirrel |
| der Igel (-) | hedgehog |
| der Fuchs (¨e) | fox |
| der Wolf (¨e) | wolf |
| der Hirsch (-e) | deer, stag |
| der Keiler (-) | wild boar |
| die Schlange (-n) | snake |
| die Schnecke (-n) | snail, slug |
| der Regenwurm (¨er) | earthworm |
| der Frosch (¨e) | frog |
| die Kröte (-n) | toad |
| die Fledermaus (¨e) | bat |
| der Affe (-n, -n) | monkey |
| der Elefant (-en, en) | elephant |
| der Löwe (-n, -n) | lion |
| der Tiger (-) | tiger |
| die Giraffe (-n) | giraffe |
| das Krokodil (-e) | crocodile |
| das Nashorn (¨er) | rhinoceros |
| das Nilpferd (-e) | hippopotamus |

| das Kamel (-e) | camel |
| der Bär (-en, -en) | bear |
| das Känguruh (-s) | kangaroo |

| das Insekt (-en) | insect |
| die Ameise (-n) | ant |
| die Fliege (-n) | fly |
| die Biene (-n) | bee |
| die Wespe (-n) | wasp |
| die Mücke (-n) | mosquito |
| summen | to buzz |
| die Spinne (-n) | spider |
| der Schmetterling (-e) | butterfly |

| das Maul (¨-er) | mouth (of animal) |
| der Schnabel (¨) | beak |
| die Feder (-n) | feather |
| der Flügel (-) | wing |
| der Schwanz (¨e) | tail |
| das Nest (-er) | nest |

## Jetzt bist du dran! 38

*Man kann hier Wörter über das Land finden. Man liest nach oben oder nach unten, vorwärts oder rückwärts. Wenn du über 30 findest, ist das sehr gut.*

*Find words about the countryside. They read up or down, forwards or backwards. If you find more than 30 you are doing very well.*

| D | O | R | F | S | Z | B | O | C | K | G | E |
| U | F | E | R | A | I | A | E | N | E | I | B |
| F | O | H | N | R | E | U | A | B | T | P | E |
| H | O | C | G | G | G | E | H | A | F | F | N |
| E | M | I | E | T | E | R | Ü | C | A | E | E |
| C | M | E | B | A | S | N | G | H | H | L | S |
| K | A | N | I | N | C | H | E | N | C | D | E |
| E | L | Ü | R | N | H | A | L | E | S | N | I |
| B | E | R | G | E | E | U | L | S | D | U | W |
| V | O | G | E | L | U | S | A | T | N | A | E |
| K | U | H | U | H | N | E | T | L | A | Z | G |
| B | R | Ü | C | K | E | E | S | D | L | A | W |

# 3 Das Wetter und das Klima — Weather and climate

| | |
|---|---|
| das Wetter | weather |
| das Klima | climate |
| das Sauwetter | filthy weather |
| herrlich | marvellous |
| der Himmel | sky |
| der Stern (-e) | star |
| der Mond | moon |
| der Schatten (-) | shade, shadow |
| die Sonne | sun |
| aufgehen* (er geht ... auf) (s; sep) | to rise |
| untergehen* (er geht ... unter) (s; sep) | to set |
| scheinen (er scheint) (s) | to shine |
| der Sonnenschein | sunshine |
| sonnig | sunny |
| der Wetterbericht (-e) | weather report |
| die Wettervorhersage (-n) | weather forecast |
| die Wetterlage | weather situation |
| die Temperatur (-en) | temperature |
| die Tageshöchsttemperatur (-en) | highest temperature of the day |
| die Tagestiefsttemperatur (-en) | lowest temperature of the day |
| Celsius | Celsius, centigrade |
| der Grad (-) | degree |
| minus drei Grad / drei Grad Kälte | minus three degrees |
| plus drei Grad | plus three degrees |
| zeitweise | at times |
| veränderlich | changeable |
| wechselnd | changeable, variable |
| die Front (-en) | front |
| der Hochdruck | high pressure |
| der Tiefdruck | low pressure |
| herrschen | to predominate |
| der Niederschlag | precipitation |
| weiterhin bewölkt | continuing cloudy |
| die Hitze | heat |
| die Kälte | cold |

| | |
|---|---|
| **heiß** | hot |
| **warm** | warm |
| **kühl** | cool |
| **kalt** | cold |
| **mild** | mild |
| **schwül** | muggy |
| **heiter** | bright |
| **die Aufheiterung (-en)** | bright period |
| | |
| **der Wind (-e)** | wind |
| **windig** | windy |
| **blasen (er bläst) (s)** | to blow |
| **stark** | strong |
| **schwach** | weak |
| **leicht** | light |
| | |
| **der Regen** | rain |
| **regnen** | to rain |
| **regnerisch** | rainy |
| **der Schauer (-)** | shower |
| **vereinzelt** | occasional, isolated |
| **nieseln** | to drizzle |
| **der Sturm (¨e)** | storm |
| **der Regensturm/Schneesturm** | rain/snow storm |
| **stürmisch** | stormy |
| **naß** | wet |
| **feucht** | damp |
| **trocken** | dry |
| **die Wolke (-n)** | cloud |
| **wolkenlos** | cloudless |
| **wolkig** / **bewölkt** | cloudy |
| **die Bewölkung** | cloud-cover |
| **bedeckt** | overcast |
| **trüb** | dull |
| | |
| **der Schnee** | snow |
| **schneien** | to snow |
| **der Schneeregen** | sleet |
| **der Hagel** | hail |
| **hageln** | to hail |
| **fallen\* (er fällt) (s)** | to fall |
| **der Frost** | frost |
| **frostig** | frosty |

| | |
|---|---|
| **frieren (es friert) (s)** | to freeze |
| **das Eis** | ice |
| **das Glatteis** | black ice |
| **glatt** | smooth |
| **glitschig** | slippery |

| | |
|---|---|
| **das Gewitter (-)** | thunderstorm |
| **der Blitz (-e)** | lightning |
| **blitzen** | to lighten |
| **der Donner** | thunder |
| **donnern** | to thunder |
| **der Nebel** | fog, mist |
| **neb(e)lig** | foggy, misty |

| | |
|---|---|
| **die Hitzewelle (-n)** | heatwave |
| **die Dürre** | drought |
| **der Brand (∸e)** | fire (*eg in forest*) |
| **die Überschwemmung (-en)** | flood |
| **das Gebiet ist überschwemmt** | the area is flooded |
| **das Erdbeben** | earthquake |
| **der Orkan (-e)** | hurricane |
| **der Tornado (-s)** | tornado |

## Jetzt bist du dran! 39

*Die Anfangsbuchstaben für die englischen Wörter bilden ein deutsches Wort, das mit dem Wetter zu tun hat, und das in England auch nicht unbekannt ist!*

*The initials for these English words make a German word, which is something to do with the weather, and is not unknown in England either!*

1 die Vorhersage:   the _ _ _ _ _ _ _

2 aufgehen:   to _ _ _ _

3 bedeckt:   _ _ _ _ _ _ _ _

4 der Himmel:   the _ _ _

5 das Gewitter:   the _ _ _ _ _ _ _ _ _ _ _

## Jetzt bist du dran! 40

Fülle die Lücken aus! Unten sind
die möglichen Lösungen, aber
alphabetisch geordnet, und mehr
Wörter als du brauchst!

Fill in the gaps. The possible
solutions are at the end, but
listed alphabetically and there
are more words than you need.

1  Es ist ja zu heiß; setz dich in den ___!
2  Morgen früh regnet es, aber ___ kommen später vom Westen.
3  Der Wind war in der Nacht sehr ___.
4  Der ___ hat den alten Baum getroffen.
5  Bei dem ___ konnten wir keine fünfzig Meter sehen.
6  Nach der ___ soll es morgen bis zu dreißig Grad ___ warm werden.
7  Heute Nacht hat es geregnet und dann ___, und es gibt ___ auf
   den Straßen.
8  Wir hatten seit zwei Monaten keinen ___, und das Gras ist ganz
   ___.
9  Ich will heute nicht spazieren gehen; der Himmel ist sehr ___.
10 Wir hatten einen kurzen ___, aber jetzt ___ die Sonne wieder.

AUFHEITERUNGEN BEWÖLKT BLITZ FEUCHT GEBLASEN GEFROREN
GLATTEIS NEBEL REGEN SCHAUER SCHEINT SCHATTEN STARK
STÜRMISCH TROCKEN TRÜB WERDEN WETTERVORHERSAGE

## 4 Umweltverschmutzung  Pollution

| | |
|---|---|
| der Mensch (-en, -en) | man, human being |
| das menschliche Leben | human life |
| die Erde | earth (*planet or soil*) |
| der Boden | ground |
| das Grundwasser | ground-water |
| die Welt | world |
| die Umwelt | environment |
| umweltfreundlich | environmentally friendly |
| umweltfeindlich | environmentally damaging |
| die Atmosphäre | atmosphere |
| schützen | to protect |

| | |
|---|---|
| **der Schmutz** | dirt |
| **verschmutzen** | to pollute |
| **die Verschmutzung** | pollution |
| **(un)rein** | (im)pure |
| **das Gift (-e)** | poison |
| **giftig** | poisonous |
| **schaden (+Dat)** | to damage |
| **der Schaden (")** | damage |
| **der Schadstoff (-e)** | harmful substance |
| **verursachen (insep)** | to cause |
| **drohen (+Dat)** | to threaten |
| **bedroht** | threatened |
| **der Stoff (-e)** | material |
| **der Rohstoff (-e)** | raw material |
| | |
| **die Spraydose (-n)** | spray-can, aerosol |
| **die Abgase (pl)** | exhaust, emission |
| **die Emission** | emission |
| **der saure Regen** | acid rain |
| **der Waldsterben** | destruction of forests by acid rain |
| **der Treibhauseffekt** | greenhouse effect |
| **das Ozonloch (")er)** | hole in ozone layer |
| **die Ozonschicht (-en)** | ozone layer |
| **die Verdünnung (-en)** | thinning |
| **zerstören (insep)** | to destroy |
| **der FCKW (-s)** | CFC |
| | |
| **sparen** | to save |
| **sparsam** | economical |
| **die Energie** | energy |
| **das Öl** | oil |
| **bleifreies Benzin** | unleaded petrol |
| **verbleites Benzin** | leaded petrol |
| | |
| **der Müll** | rubbish |
| **die Mülltonne** | dustbin |
| **die Mülldeponie (-n)** | waste disposal site |
| **der Altglascontainer (-)** | bottle bank |
| **der Problem-Müll** | problem refuse (batteries, oil, etc) |
| **der Sperrmüll** | bulky items of refuse |
| **recyceln** | to recycle |
| **das Recycling** | recycling |

| der Kunststoff (-e) } das Plastik } | plastic |
| das Papier | paper |
| das Altpapier | waste paper |
| das Metall (-e) | metal |
| das Altmetall | scrap metal |

## 5 Das Verbrechen — Crime

### a Der Diebstahl — Theft

| das Verbrechen (-) | crime |
| der Verbrecher (-) | criminal |
| der Diebstahl (¨e) | theft |
| der Dieb (-e) | thief |
| der Taschendieb (-e) | pick-pocket |

| der Überfall (¨e) | robbery, attack |
| überfallen (er überfällt) (s; insep) | to hold up, attack |
| eine Bank ausrauben (sep) | to rob a bank |
| einbrechen* (in +Acc) (er bricht ein) (s; sep) | to break in |
| sie sind ins Geschäft eingebrochen | they broke into the shop |
| der Einbruch (¨e) | burglary, break-in |
| der Einbrecher (-) | burglar (m) |
| die Einbrecherin (-nen) | burglar (f) |
| die Maske (-n) | mask |
| maskiert | masked |

| stehlen (er stiehlt) (s) | to steal |
| fliehen* (er flieht) (s) | to flee |
| den Alarm auslösen (sep) | to set off the alarm |
| die Polizei alarmieren | to alert the police |
| verhaften (insep) | to arrest |
| die Sirene (-n) | siren |
| das Martinshorn | German police/fire siren |

### b Die Gewalt — Violence

| Hände hoch! | hands up! |
| bewaffnet | armed |
| die Waffe (-n) | weapon, gun |
| die Pistole (-n) | pistol |

| | |
|---|---|
| schießen (er schießt) (*s*) | to shoot |
| bedrohen (*insep*) | to threaten |
| erschrecken (er erschrickt) (*s; insep*) | to be frightened |
| erschrecken (w) | to frighten |
| schlagen (er schlägt) (*s*) | to beat, hit |
| zusammenschlagen (*s; sep*) | to beat up |
| der Raubüberfall (¨e) | mugging |
| der Straßenräuber (-) | mugger |
| der blaue Fleck (-e *or* -en) | bruise |
| die Vergewaltigung (-en) | rape |
| der Mord (-e) | murder |
| der Mörder (-)/die Mörderin (-nen) | murderer (*m/f*) |
| tot | dead |
| töten umbringen (er bringt ... um) (*irr w; sep*) | to kill |
| umkommen* (er kommt ... um) (*s; sep*) sterben* (er stirbt) (*s*) | to die |

## c Die Deliquenz — Delinquency

| | |
|---|---|
| schwänzen | to play truant |
| der Rowdy (-s) | hooligan, vandal |
| das Rowdytum | hooliganism |
| beschädigen (*insep*) | to vandalise |
| raufen | to fight, scrap |
| betrunken werden* (*s*) | to get drunk |
| Langeweile (*f*) haben | to be bored |
| keine Zukunft haben | to have no future |
| er hat keine Aussicht auf Arbeit | he has no hope of work |

## d Recht und Ordnung — Law and order

| | |
|---|---|
| die Polizei | police |
| der Polizist (-en, -en) | policeman |
| die Polizistin (-nen) | policewoman |
| der Detektiv (-e)/die Detektivin (-nen) | private detective (*m/f*) |
| auf Streife sein* | to be on patrol |
| bewaffnet sein* | to be armed |
| Nachforschungen anstellen (*sep*) | to make enquiries |
| der Fingerabdruck (¨e) | finger print |
| die Spur (-en) | clue |

| | |
|---|---|
| das **Phantombild** (-er) | photofit picture |
| **verdächtigen** (*insep*) | to suspect |
| der/die **Verdächtige** (*adj. noun*) | suspect |
| **verhaften** | to arrest |
| der **Haftbefehl** (-e) | arrest warrant |
| **vernehmen** (er **vernimmt**) (s; *insep*) | to question |
| **anklagen** (*sep*) | to charge |
| die **Aussage** (-n) | statement |
| der **Zeuge** (-n, -n) }<br>die **Zeugin** (-nen) } | witness (*m/f*) |
| die **Belohnung** (-en) | reward |

| | |
|---|---|
| das **Gericht** (-e) | court |
| die **Strafe** (-n) | fine, punishment |
| der **Richter** (-) }<br>die **Richterin** (-nen) } | judge (*m/f*) |
| die **Schöffen** (*pl*) }<br>die **Geschworenen** (*pl*) } | jury |
| das **Urteil** (-e) | verdict |
| **schuldig/unschuldig** | guilty/innocent |
| das **Gefängnis** | prison |
| er kam ins **Gefängnis** | he went to prison |
| die **Begnadigung** (-en) | pardon |

## 6 *Das Einkaufen*    *Shopping*

### a Taschengeld ausgeben    Spending pocket money

| | |
|---|---|
| **bekommen** (er **bekommt**) (s; *insep*) | to get, receive |
| Ich gebe mein **Taschengeld** für ... aus | I spend my pocket money on... |
| **CDs** (*f pl*) | CDs |
| **Videos** (*n pl*) | videos |
| **Sport** (*m*) | sport |
| **Schminke** (*f*) | make-up |
| **Bücher** (*n pl*) | books |
| **Reisen** (*n pl*) | travelling |

### b Die Läden    Shops

| | |
|---|---|
| der **Laden** (⸚) | shop |
| das **Geschäft** (-e) | shop, business |
| das **Warenhaus** (⸚er) }<br>das **Kaufhaus** (⸚er) } | department store |

| | |
|---|---|
| **der Supermarkt** (¨e) | supermarket |
| **der Kiosk** (-e) | kiosk |
| | |
| **die Lebensmittel** (*pl*) | groceries |
| **das Lebensmittelgeschäft** (-e) | grocer's |
| **die Obst- und Gemüsehandlung** (-en) | greengrocer's |
| **die Fleischerei** (-en) ⎫ | |
| **die Metzgerei** (-en) ⎭ | butcher's |
| **das Fischgeschäft** (-e) | fish-monger's |
| **das Delikatessengeschäft** (-e) | delicatessen |
| **die Bäckerei** (-en) | baker's |
| **die Konditorei** (-en) | cake shop, sometimes with café |
| **der Süßwarenladen** (¨) | sweet shop, confectioner's |
| | |
| **das Bekleidungsgeschäft** (-e) | clothes shop |
| **das Schuhgeschäft** (-e) | shoe shop |
| **der Friseur** | hairdresser's |
| **das Blumengeschäft** (-e) | florist's |
| **die Apotheke** (-n) | chemist's (*for medicines*) |
| **die Drogerie** (-n) | chemist's, drug-store |
| **die (chemische) Reinigung** | (dry) cleaner's |
| **der Waschsalon** (-s) | launderette |
| **die Post** (*no pl*) ⎫ | |
| **das Postamt** (¨er) ⎭ | post office |
| **das Sportgeschäft** (¨) | sports shop |
| **der Spielwarenladen** (¨) | toy shop |
| **die Buchhandlung** (-en) | bookshop |
| **die Schreibwarenhandlung** (-en) ⎫ | |
| **das Schreibwarengeschäft** (-e) ⎭ | stationer's |
| **der Juwelier** (-e) | jeweller's |
| **der Zeitungshändler** (-) | newsagent |
| **der Zeitungsstand** (¨e) | newspaper stall |
| **der Zeitungskiosk** (-e) | newspaper kiosk |
| **die Bude** (-n) | kiosk |
| **der Tabakladen** (¨) | tobacconist's |
| **die Weinhandlung** (-en) | wine-merchant's |
| **die Bierhalle** (-n) | beerhall |
| **das Gasthaus** (¨er) | inn |
| | |
| **geöffnet** ⎫ | |
| **auf** ⎬ | open |
| **offen** ⎭ | |
| **geschlossen** ⎫ | shut |
| **zu** ⎭ | |

| aufhaben/zuhaben (*sep*) | to be open/shut |
|---|---|
| durchgehend geöffnet | open without lunch-break |
| die Geschäftszeiten (*pl*) ⎫ | |
| die Öffnungszeiten (*pl*) ⎭ | opening hours |
| (der) Feierabend | closing time |
| der Ruhetag (-e) | day when shop does not open |
| die Betriebsferien (*pl*) | annual holiday (*when business is shut*) |

## Jetzt bist du dran! 41

Schreib den Namen des Ladens, wo man jeden Artikel kaufen kann.

Write the name of the shop where you can buy each article.

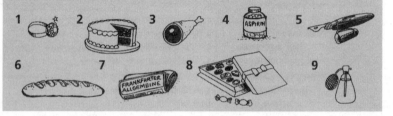

## Jetzt bist du dran! 42

In dieser Stadt gibt es noch keinen Supermarkt; du mußt all deine Einkäufe in kleineren Spezialläden machen. Zu welchen Läden mußt du gehen?

There is not supermarket in this town, so you must do all your shopping in smaller specialised shops. Which shops must you go to?

1 Du suchst ein Geschenk für eine alte Dame, Rosen zum Beispiel.
2 Du möchtest heute Brötchen essen.
3 Eure Gäste essen sehr gern Fisch, und du sollst heute einkaufen.
4 Du möchtest einen schönen, warmen Pullover.
5 Heute wollt ihr Rindfleisch essen.
6 Du mußt einen guten Füller für die Schule haben.
7 Du hast keine Papiertaschentücher mehr, und du mußt welche kaufen.
8 Du bist erkältet und hast keine Medikamente mehr.
9 Wie wäre es mit einem leckeren Erdbeerkuchen?
10 Und zu guter Letzt natürlich einige Bonbons!

## c Einkaufen (Allgemeines) — Shopping (general)

| | |
|---|---|
| verkaufen (insep) | to sell |
| einkaufen (sep) | to shop |
| der Einkauf (∵e) | purchase |
| Einkäufe machen | to go shopping |
| die Einkaufsliste (-n) | shopping list |
| der Kunde (-n, -n) }<br>die Kundin (-nen) } | customer (*m/f*) |
| | |
| Sie sind an der Reihe | it's your turn |
| kann ich Ihnen helfen? | can I help you? |
| werden Sie schon bedient? | are you being served? |
| was darf es sein? }<br>was möchten Sie? } | what would you like? |
| suchen Sie etwas Bestimmtes? | are you looking for anything in particular? |
| | |
| haben Sie (außerdem) noch Wünsche? | would you like anything else? |
| darf es sonst noch etwas sein? | will there be anything else? |
| sonst noch etwas? | anything else? |
| ich hätte/möchte gerne... | I would like... |
| führen Sie...? | do you stock...? |
| erhältlich | available, obtainable |
| die Sorte (-n) | sort |
| | |
| die Liste (-n) | list |
| brauchen | to need |
| holen | to fetch |
| suchen | to look for |
| aussuchen (*sep*) | to pick, select |
| sich erinnern an (+*Acc*) (*insep*) | to remember |
| zeigen auf (+*Acc*) | to point to |
| wählen | to choose |
| die Auswahl | selection, choice |
| drei Stück | three (of whatever item it is) |
| die Menge (-n) | crowd |
| eine Menge (+*noun*) | a lot of... |
| jede Menge (+*noun*) | masses/loads of... |
| | |
| das Schaufenster (-) | shop window |
| die Abteilung (-en) | department |
| das Erdgeschoß (im Erdgeschoß) | (on the) ground floor |
| das Untergeschoß (im Untergeschoß) | (in the) basement |

| | |
|---|---|
| im ersten Stock | on the first floor |
| die Rolltreppe (-n) | escalator |
| der Einkaufskorb (¨e) | shopping basket |
| der Korb (¨e) | basket |
| der Einkaufswagen (-) | trolley |
| der Artikel (-) | article |
| das Ding (-e) }<br>die Sache (-n) } | thing |
| die Garantie | guarantee |
| die Gebrauchsanweisung (-en) | instructions for use |
| gebrauchen | to use |
| die Anweisung (-en) | instructions |
| (sich) bedienen (*insep*) | to serve (oneself) |
| der Automat (-en, -en) | vending machine |

## d Bezahlen — Paying

| | |
|---|---|
| die Kasse (-n) | check-out, cashdesk, till |
| der Kassierer (-) | cashier (*m*) |
| die Kassiererin (-nen) | cashier (*f*) |
| der Verkäufer (-) | salesman |
| die Verkäuferin (-nen) | saleswoman |
| ausgeben (er gibt ... aus) (*s; sep*) | to spend (*money*) |
| kaufen | to buy |
| bezahlen (*insep*) | to pay (for) |
| die Bezahlung | payment |
| die Handtasche (-n) | handbag |
| das Portemonnaie (-s) }<br>der Geldbeutel (-) }<br>die Geldbörse (-n) } | purse |
| die Brieftasche (-n) | wallet |
| der Scheck (-s) | cheque |
| das Scheckbuch (¨er) | cheque book |
| mit Scheck bezahlen (*insep*) | to pay by cheque |
| die Scheckkarte (-n) | cheque card |
| die Kreditkarte (-n) | credit card |
| (in) bar bezahlen | to pay (in) cash |
| das Bargeld | cash |
| das Kleingeld | small change |
| die Münze (-n) | coin |
| der Schein (-e) | banknote |
| die Mehrwertsteuer (MwSt) | VAT |
| der Kassenzettel (-) | till receipt |

| | |
|---|---|
| **die Quittung (-en)** | receipt |
| **wieviel/was kostet...?** | what does ... cost? |
| **das macht zusammen 8 Mark** | that makes 8 DM altogether |
| **insgesamt** | altogether, in total |
| **bitte schön** | here you are |
| **einwickeln** (*sep*) } | |
| **einpacken** (*sep*) } | to wrap up |
| **die Sachen zusammenpacken** (*sep*) | to pack up the things |
| **die Packung (-en)** } | |
| **das Päckchen (-)** } | packet |
| **das Paket (-e)** | parcel |
| **die Schachtel (-n)** | box |
| **das Gummiband (¨er)** | rubber band |
| **der Tesafilm ®** | Sellotape ® |
| **die Einkaufstasche (-n)** | shopping-bag |
| **der Plastikbeutel (-)** | plastic (shopping-)bag |
| **die Tüte (-n)** | (small) paper/plastic bag |
| **einstecken** (*sep*) | to put away |
| **teuer** | expensive |
| **kostspielig** | costly |
| **billig** | cheap |
| **preiswert** | inexpensive |
| **günstig** | reasonable, a bargain |
| **verbilligt** | reduced |
| **die Preissenkung (-en)** | reduction |
| **die Hälfte (-n)** | half |
| **ich bekomme 10 Prozent Rabatt** | I get 10 per cent discount |
| **umsonst** | free, for nothing |
| **der Preis (-e)** | price |
| **der Aufkleber (-)** | sticker |
| **die Anzeige (-n)** | advert |
| **(an)bieten (er bietet ... an)** (*s; sep*) | to offer |
| **im Angebot** | on offer, reduced |
| **das Sonderangebot (-e)** | special offer |
| **der Sonderpreis (-e)** | special price |
| **der Ausverkauf** | sales |
| **etwas im Ausverkauf kaufen** | to buy something at the sales |
| **der Sommerschlußverkauf (SSV)** | autumn sales |
| **umtauschen** (*sep*) | to exchange |
| **der Umtausch** | exchange |
| **liefern** | to deliver |

## e Essen kaufen | Shopping for food

| | |
|---|---|
| wiegen (er wiegt) (s) | to weigh |
| das Gewicht (-e) | weight |
| das Gramm (g) | gramme |
| das Kilo(gramm) (kg) | kilo(gramme) |
| pro Kilo | per kilo |
| etwa/ungefähr zwei Kilo | about 2 kg |
| das Pfund | (German) pound (500 g) |
| ein halbes Pfund | half a (German) pound |
| nur | only |
| wieviel möchten Sie? | how much would you like? |
| wie viele möchten Sie? | how many would you like? |
| darf es ein bißchen mehr sein? | do you mind if it's a little over? |
| genug | enough |
| zuwenig/zuviel | too little/too much |
| einige | some |
| etwas (Käse) | a little (cheese) |
| ein paar | a few |
| verkaufen Sie die Äpfel einzeln? | do you sell the apples singly? |
| die Scheibe (-n) | slice |
| im Stück oder geschnitten? | in a lump or sliced? |
| das Glas (¨er) | jar |
| die Dose (-n) | tin |

| | |
|---|---|
| frisch | fresh |
| kühl aufbewahren | store in a cool place |
| das Mindesthaltbarkeitsdatum | best-before date |
| mindestens haltbar bis Ende Juni 1999 | best before end of June 1999 |

## f Getränke kaufen | Shopping for drink

| | |
|---|---|
| die Flasche (-n) | bottle |
| die Literflasche (-n) | 1-litre bottle |
| der/das Liter (-) (l) | litre |
| die Plastikflasche (-n) | plastic bottle |
| die Einwegflasche (-n) | non-returnable bottle |
| die Mehrwegflasche (-n) <br> die Pfandflasche (-n) } | returnable bottle |
| auf der Flasche ist 30 Pf Pfand | the bottle has a 30 Pf deposit |
| die Packung (-en) | carton (eg of milk) |

## g Kleidung kaufen — Shopping for clothes

| | |
|---|---|
| anprobieren (sep) | to try on |
| die Farbe (-n) | colour |
| die Größe (-n) | size |
| die Nummer (-n) (Nr) | number (no), size |
| eine Nummer größer | one size larger |
| passen (+*Dat*) | to fit |
| das paßt mir nicht | that doesn't fit me |
| das steht mir nicht | that doesn't suit me |
| die Anprobe (-n) | fitting room |
| eng | small, tight |
| weit | large, wide |
| lang | long |
| kurz | short |

| | |
|---|---|
| die Mode (-n) | fashion |
| ...ist jetzt große Mode | ...is very fashionable nowadays |
| (un)modisch | (un)fashionable |
| schick | elegant, smart, chic |
| empfehlen (er empfiehlt) (*s*) | to recommend |

| | |
|---|---|
| der Stoff (-e) | cloth |
| die Wolle | wool |
| die Baumwolle | cotton |
| die Seide | silk |
| das Leder | leather |
| das Wildleder | suede |
| der Kunststoff } das Plastik } | plastic |
| das Gummi | rubber |
| aus Seide usw | made of silk etc |
| echt | genuine |
| die Qualität (-en) | quality |
| fein | fine, delicate |
| gestreift | striped |
| kariert | checked |

See also Colours, page 183.

## Jetzt bist du dran! 43

Unten sind die möglichen Lösungen, aber alphabetisch geordnet, und mehr Wörter als du brauchst!

The possible solutions are at the end, but listed alphabetically and more words than you need!

1  Wenn man zunimmt, wird die Jeans etwas ___.
2  Wenn man sein Scheckbuch vergessen hat, muß man ___ zahlen.
3  Die Verkäuferin fragte mich: ‚Was ___ es sein, bitte?'
4  Die Bananen sehen lecker aus; ich möchte vier ___ kaufen!
5  Der Pullover ist etwas weit für mich; ich möchte eine ___ kleiner, bitte.
6  ‚Sie haben so viele Äpfel; welche ___ Sie?'
7  ‚Wo ist die ___ für Uhren, bitte?'
8  ‚Sie müssen an der ___ zahlen.'
9  ‚Wir müssen uns beeilen; das Geschäft wird um 18 Uhr ___.'
10  ‚Wir haben von 8 bis 18 Uhr ___ geöffnet!'
11  ‚Da sind die Kekse, die Sie suchen; ___ Sie sich doch!'
12  ‚Bitte schön; diese Broschüre bekommen Sie ___.'
13  ‚Dieser Pullover paßt mir ja gar nicht; ich muß ihn ___.'
14  ‚Welche Pralinen meinen Sie? ___ Sie darauf!'
15  ‚Das ist mir etwas zu teuer; ich möchte nicht so viel ___.'

---

ABTEILUNG AUSGEBEN AUSSUCHEN BAR BEDIENEN DARF DURCHGEHEND EMPFEHLEN ENG GESCHLOSSEN KASSE NUMMER SCHAUFENSTER STÜCK UMSONST UMTAUSCHEN VERKAUFEN WEIT WIEGEN ZEIGEN

---

### h Die Kleider — Clothes

| | |
|---|---|
| die Kleider (pl) | clothes, clothing |
| die Herrenkonfektion | men's wear |
| die Damenkonfektion | ladies' wear |
| die Herren-/Damenmode (-n) | gentlemen's/ladies' fashion |
| die Sachen (pl) | things, gear |
| der Hut (¨e) | hat |
| die Mütze (-n) | cap |
| der Handschuh (-e) | glove |

| | |
|---|---|
| der Mantel (⁓) | coat |
| der Regenmantel (⁓) | raincoat |
| der (Regen)schirm (-e) | umbrella |
| der Anorak (-s) | anorak |
| die Jacke (-n) | jacket (loose, casual) |
| das/der Sakko (-s) | sports jacket |
| der Anzug (⁓e) | suit |
| das Kostüm (-e) | suit (*woman's*) |
| die Bluse (-n) | blouse |
| das Hemd (-en) | shirt |
| die Krawatte (-n) }<br>der Schlips (-e) } | tie |
| das T-Shirt (-s) | T-shirt |
| der Pullover (-) }<br>der Pulli (-s) } | pullover |
| der Pullunder (-) | tank-top, sleeveless pullover |
| die Strickjacke (-n) | cardigan |
| der Schal (-e *or* -s) | scarf/shawl |
| das Kleid (-er) | dress |
| der Rock (⁓e) | skirt |
| die Wäsche/Unterwäsche | underwear |
| das Unterhemd (-en) | vest |
| die Unterhose (-n) | pants |
| das Höschen (-) | pants (*f*) |
| der Slip (-s) | knickers |
| der Büstenhalter (-)/der BH (-s) | bra |
| die Hose (-n) | (pair of) trousers |
| die Jeans (*sg/pl*) | (pair of) jeans |
| die Shorts (*sg/pl*) | (pair of) shorts |
| die Tasche (-n) | pocket |
| das Taschentuch/<br>Papiertaschentuch (⁓er) } | (paper) handkerchief |
| der Gürtel (-) | belt |
| der Hosenträger (-) | (pair of) braces |
| die Socke (-n) | sock |
| der Strumpf (⁓e) | stocking |
| die Strumpfhose (-n) | (pair of) tights |
| der Schuh (-e) | shoe |
| das Paar Schuhe | pair of shoes |
| der Sportschuh (-e) | trainer |
| der Hallenschuh (-e) | gym shoe |
| die Sandale (-n) | sandal |
| der Hausschuh (-e) | slipper, indoor shoe |
| der Pantoffel (-n) | (bedroom) slipper |

| | |
|---|---|
| der Stiefel (-) | boot |
| der Gummistiefel (-) | wellington boot |
| der Trainingsanzug (¨e) } der Jogginganzug (¨e) } | track suit |
| der Schlafanzug (¨e) } der Pyjama (-s) } | pair of pyjamas |
| das Nachthemd (-en) | nightdress |

## Jetzt bist du dran! 44

| *Was ist das?* | *What is that?* |
|---|---|
| 1 | d _ _ _ _ _ _ _ |
| 2 | d _ _ _ _ _ _ _ |
| 3 | d _ _ _ _ _ _ |
| 4 | d _ _ _ _ _ |
| 5 | d _ _ _ _ _ |
| 6 | d _ _ _ _ _ _ _ _ _ _ _ |
| 7 | d _ _ _ _ _ _ _ _ _ |
| 8 | d _ _ _ _ _ _ |
| 9 | d _ _ _ _ _ _ _ |
| 10 | d _ _ _ _ _ _ |
| 11 | d _ _ _ _ _ |
| 12 | d _ _ _ _ _ _ _ |

## i Sonstiges — Other items

| | |
|---|---|
| der Schmuck | jewellery |
| das Gold | gold |

| | |
|---|---|
| **das Silber** | silver |
| **die Armbanduhr (-en)** | wristwatch |
| **die Kette (-n)** | chain |
| **die Halskette (-n)** | necklace |
| **der Ring (-e)** | ring |
| **der Stein (-e)** | stone |
| **die Brille (-n)** | pair of glasses |

| | |
|---|---|
| **die Schminke (-n)** | make-up |
| **der Lippenstift (-e)** | lipstick |
| **das Parfüm (-e)** | perfume |

| | |
|---|---|
| **die Zeitung (-en)** | newspaper |
| **die Zeitschrift (-en)** | magazine, periodical |
| **der Tabak** | tobacco |
| **die Zigarette (-n)** | cigarette |
| **die Zigarre (-n)** | cigar |
| **die Pfeife (-n)** | pipe |
| **haben Sie Feuer?** | have you got a light? |
| **das Streichholz (-̈er)** | match |
| **das Feuerzeug (-e)** | lighter |
| **anzünden (*sep*)** | to light |
| **rauchen** | to smoke |

## j Die chemische Reinigung

## The dry cleaner's

| | |
|---|---|
| **reinigen** | to clean |
| **ich möchte diese Hose reinigen lassen** | I'd like to get this pair of trousers cleaned |
| **der Fleck (-e *or* -en)** | spot, stain |
| **bügeln** | to iron |
| **flicken** ⎫<br>**ausbessern (*sep*)** ⎬ | to repair |
| **das Loch (-̈er)** | hole |
| **nähen** | to sew |
| **annähen (*sep*)** | to sew on |
| **der Knopf (-̈e)** | button |
| **der Klettverschluß (-üsse)** | velcro ® fastening |
| **der Reißverschluß (-üsse)** | zip |
| **können Sie es bis 3 Uhr machen?** | can you do it by 3 o'clock? |
| **es eilt nicht** ⎫<br>**es hat Zeit** ⎬ | there's no hurry |
| **abholen (*sep*)** | to collect, pick up |

## k Die Bank     The bank

| | |
|---|---|
| die Bank (-en) <br> die Sparkasse (-n) } | bank |
| das Konto (Konten) | account |
| die Kontonummer (-n) | account number |
| das Geld | money |
| sparen | to save |
| Geld abheben (er hebt ... ab) (s; sep) | to take out money |
| Geld überweisen (er überweist) (s; insep) | to transfer money |
| der Scheck (-s) | cheque |
| der Reisescheck (-s or -e) | traveller's cheque |
| die Scheckkarte (-n) | cheque card |
| das Scheckbuch (-er) | cheque book |
| ein Scheck über DM 100 | a cheque for DM 100 |
| einen Scheck einlösen (sep) | to cash a cheque |
| die Gebühr (-en) | fee, commission |
| die Eurokarte (-n) | cash card |
| | |
| der Ausweis (-e) | identity card |
| sich ausweisen (er weist sich aus) (s; sep) | to produce identification |
| der Paß/Reisepaß (Pässe) | passport |
| vorzeigen (sep) | to show/produce |
| | |
| die Wechselstube (-n) | bureau de change |
| wechseln | to change (money) |
| die Währung (-en) | currency |
| der Kurs/Wechselkurs (-e) | exchange rate |
| der Geldwechsel | exchange of money |
| | |
| der Schein/Geldschein (-e) | banknote |
| der Fünfzigmarkschein (-e) | DM 50 note |
| das Bargeld | cash |
| bar bezahlen | to pay cash |
| die Münze (-n) | coin |
| das Kleingeld | (small) change |
| die Deutsche Mark (DM) | Deutschmark |
| der Pfennig (-) | hundredth of a Mark |
| der Schilling (-) | Austrian schilling |
| der Groschen (-) | { hundredth of Schilling (Austria) <br> 10 Pfennig piece (Germany) |

| | |
|---|---|
| der Franken (-) | Swiss franc |
| der Rappen (-) | Swiss centime |
| das Pfund (-) | pound (*£1 or 1 lb*) |
| der Franc (-s) | French/Belgian franc |
| der Dollar (-s) | dollar |

## I Das Postamt — The post office

| | |
|---|---|
| die Post (*no pl*) }<br>das Postamt (¨er) } | post office |
| der Schalter (-) | counter, window |
| die Schlange (-n) | queue |
| Schlange stehen (*s*) }<br>anstehen (er steht ... an) (*s; sep*) } | to queue |
| ich bin jetzt dran }<br>Ich komme jetzt dran } | it's my turn now |
| schicken | to send |
| der Brief (-e) | letter |
| der Umschlag (¨e) | envelope |
| die Briefmarke (-n) | stamp |
| das Postwertzeichen (-) | stamp (*official word*) |
| aufkleben (*sep*) | to stick on |
| zehn Briefmarken zu einer Mark | ten 1 DM stamps |
| der Briefmarkenautomat (-en, -en) | stamp vending machine |
| die Geldrückgabe | returned coins |
| Geld einwerfen (er wirft ... ein)<br>(*s; sep*) | to put in money |
| außer Betrieb | out of order |
| die Postleitzahl | post code |
| der Absender (-) (Abs.) | sender (*The sender's name and address are always written on the envelope in Germany.*) |
| der Briefträger (-) | postman |
| die Briefträgerin (-nen) | postwoman |
| der Briefkasten (¨) | postbox |
| einen Brief einwerfen (*s; sep*) | to post a letter |
| in den Briefkasten werfen | to post |
| einen Brief/ein Paket aufgeben<br>(er gibt ... auf) (*s; sep*) | to post a letter/parcel |
| der Einwurf | coin slot; postbox opening |
| leeren | to empty |
| die Leerung (-en) | collection (*of post from box*) |
| der Eilbrief (-e) | urgent letter |
| eingeschrieben | registered |

| | |
|---|---|
| **postlagernd** | poste restante |
| **die Luftpost** | airmail |
| **mit Luftpost** | by airmail |
| **das Inland** | home (*ie not abroad*) |
| **das Ausland** | abroad |
| **das Telegramm (-e)** | telegramme |
| **die Postanweisung (-en)** | postal order (*approx*) |
| **einlösen (*sep*)** | to cash |

For telephone information see Telephoning, pages 167–8.
See also Letters, pages 166–7.

## m Das Fundbüro — Lost property office

| | |
|---|---|
| **verlieren (er verliert) (*s; insep*)** | to lose |
| **lassen (er läßt) (*s*)** | to leave |
| **liegenlassen (er läßt ... liegen) (*s; sep*)** | to leave behind |
| **abgeben (er gibt ... ab) (*s; sep*)** | to hand in |
| **der Artikel (-)** | article |
| **wertvoll** | valuable |
| **das Formular (-e)** | form |
| **ausfüllen (*sep*)** | to fill in |
| **beschreiben (er beschreibt) (*s; insep*)** | to describe |
| **die Beschreibung (-en)** | description |
| **gehören (+*Dat*) (*insep*)** | to belong to |
| **der Dieb (-e)** | thief |
| **der Taschendieb (-e)** | pickpocket |
| **stehlen (er stiehlt) (*s*)** | to steal |
| **klauen (*colloquial*)** | to pinch |
| **verschwinden\* (er verschwindet) (*s; insep*)** | to disappear |

## 7 Fahren und Fahrzeuge Travel and transport

### a Allgemeines — General

| | |
|---|---|
| **reisen\*** | to travel |
| **losfahren\* (*s; sep*)** | to set off |
| **verreisen\* (*insep*)** | to go away on a journey |
| **abreisen (*sep*)** | to leave |
| **die Fahrt (-en)** | journey |

| | |
|---|---|
| **der/die Reisende** (*adj. noun*) | traveller |
| **abfahren** (*s; sep*) | to depart |
| **ankommen** (*s; sep*) | to arrive |
| **pünktlich** | on time, punctual(ly) |
| **verspätet** | late |
| | |
| **der Verkehr** | traffic |
| **der Lärm** | noise |
| **die Panne** (-n) | breakdown |
| **langsam** | slow(ly) |
| **schnell** | fast |
| **vorne** | in the front |
| **hinten** | in the back |
| **warten auf** (+*Acc*) | to wait for |
| **die Grenze** (-n) | border |
| **der Paß** (Pässe) | passport |
| **die Paßkontrolle** (-n) | passport control |
| **der Zoll** | customs |
| **die Zollkontrolle** (-n) | customs inspection |
| **der Zollbeamte** (*adj. noun*) | customs officer |
| **verzollen** (*insep*) | to declare at customs |
| **schmuggeln** | to smuggle |
| **der Schmuggler** (-) | smuggler |
| **zollfreie Waren** (*pl*) | duty-free goods |
| **der Alkohol** (-) | alcohol |
| **das Parfüm** (-e *or* -s) | perfume |
| **die Zigaretten** (*f pl*) | cigarettes |
| **das Gepäck** | luggage |
| **das Gepäck abgeben** (er gibt ... ab) (*s; sep*) | to give in one's luggage |

## b Der Individualverkehr — Private transport

| | |
|---|---|
| **das Fahrrad/Rad** (¨-er) | bicycle |
| **radfahren*** (er fährt Rad) (*s; sep*) | to ride a bicycle |
| **wo kann ich mein Fahrrad abstellen?** | where can I leave my bike? |
| **der Radweg** (-e) | cycle track |
| | |
| **der Roller** (-) | motor scooter |
| **das Mofa** (-s) | (*low powered*) moped |
| **das Moped** (-s) | moped |
| **das Motorrad** (¨-er) | motor cycle |

| | |
|---|---|
| der Radfahrer / Motorradfahrer (-) | (motor) cyclist (*m*) |
| die Radfahrerin/ Motorradfahrerin (-nen) | (motor) cyclist (*f*) |
| der Schutzhelm (-e) | helmet |
| das Fahrzeug (-e) | vehicle |
| das Auto (-s) / der Wagen (-) | car |
| das Kfz (-s) (Kraftfahrzeug (-e)) | motor vehicle |
| der Pkw (-s) (Personenkraftwagen) (-) | car (*formal word*) |
| das Taxi (-s) | taxi |
| der Lkw (-s) (Lastkraftwagen) (-) | lorry |
| der Lieferwagen (-) | delivery lorry |
| die Limousine (-n) | saloon car |
| der Kombi (-s) | estate car |
| das Kabrio/Kabriolett (-s) | convertible |
| der Sportwagen (-) | sports car |
| die Marke (-n) | make |
| der Ford (usw) | the Ford (*and all makes of car*) |
| Auto fahren (er fährt Auto) (s) | to be a car driver |
| der Fahrer (-)/die Fahrerin (-nen) | driver (*m/f*) |
| der Mitfahrer (-) | passenger (*m*) |
| die Mitfahrerin (-nen) | passenger (*f*) |
| die Politesse (-n) | traffic warden (*f*) |
| der Polizist (-en, -en) | policeman |
| die Polizistin (-nen) | policewoman |
| die Fahrprüfung machen | to take one's driving test |
| der Führerschein (-e) | driving licence |
| die Autokarte (-n) | road map |
| der Motor (-en) | engine |
| ich lasse den Motor an | I start up the engine |
| der Motor springt an | the engine starts |
| der Kühler (-) | radiator |
| die Zündkerze (-n) | spark plug |
| die Batterie (-n) | battery |
| die Kupplung | clutch |
| das Getriebe (-) | gear box |
| der Gang (¨e) | gear |
| die Bremse (-n) | brake |
| bremsen | to brake |

| | |
|---|---|
| die Haube/Motorhaube (-n) | bonnet |
| der Kofferraum (¨e) | boot |
| das Auspuffrohr (-e) | exhaust pipe |
| der Katalysator (-en) | catalytic convertor |
| der Scheinwerfer (-) | headlight |
| das Standlicht (-er) | sidelight |
| mit Abblendlicht fahren* (s) | to drive with dipped headlights |
| die Windschutzscheibe (-n) | windscreen |
| der Scheibenwischer (-) | windscreen wiper |
| das Steuer (-) | steering wheel |
| mein Bruder saß am Steuer | my brother was at the wheel |
| die Links-/Rechtssteuerung | left/right-hand drive |
| der Rückspiegel (-) | driving mirror |
| das Rad (¨er) | wheel |
| das Vorderrad/Hinterrad (¨er) | front/rear wheel |
| wechseln | to change |
| das Nummernschild (-er) | number plate |
| das amtliche Kennzeichen | registration number |
| die Stoßstange (-n) | bumper |
| der Gurt/Sicherheitsgurt (-e) | seat-belt |
| anlegen (sep) | to fasten |
| sich anschnallen (sep) | to put on one's seat-belt |
| die Hupe (-n) | horn |
| hupen | to sound the horn |
| der Benzintank (-s or -e) | petrol tank |

## c Unterwegs — On the road

| | |
|---|---|
| sie lernt Auto fahren | she's learning to drive |
| fahren* (er fährt) (s) | to drive |
| die Fahrschule (-n) | driving school |
| der Fahrlehrer (-) | driving instructor (m) |
| die Fahrlehrerin (-nen) | driving instructor (f) |
| der Fahrschüler (-) | learner driver (m) |
| die Fahrschülerin (-nen) | learner driver (f) |
| die Straßenverkehrsordnung | highway code |
| die Fahrprüfung machen | to take the driving test |
| vorwärts | forwards |
| rückwärts | backwards |

| | |
|---|---|
| das Schild (-er) | sign |
| die Ampel (-n) | traffic light |
| bei Rot über die Ampel fahren | to go through the red light |

| | |
|---|---|
| der Bahnübergang (¨e) | level crossing |
| der Fußgängerübergang (¨e) | pedestrian crossing |
| | |
| keine Einfahrt | no entry |
| die Einbahnstraße (-n) | one-way street |
| Anlieger frei | no thoroughfare – residents only |
| Ausfahrt freihalten | driveway – keep clear |
| Abstand halten | keep your distance |
| Schritt fahren | dead slow |
| Vorfahrt beachten | give way |
| Vorsicht bei Nässe | care when roads wet |
| die Vorfahrt | priority |
| die Warnung (-en) | warning |
| Achtung! | attention/watch out! |
| achten auf (+Acc) | to pay attention to |
| | |
| parken | to park |
| der Parkplatz (¨e) | car-park; parking space |
| das Parkhaus (¨er) | multi-storey car-park |
| die Parkuhr (-en) | parking meter |
| die Politesse (-n) | traffic warden (f) |
| der Parkschein (-e) | parking permit |
| das Parkverbot | no-parking area |
| | |
| der Stau (-e or -s) | traffic jam |
| der Durchgangsverkehr | through traffic |
| die Hauptverkehrszeit (-en) | rush-hour |
| die Umleitung (-en) | diversion |
| die Geschwindigkeit (-en) | speed |
| die Geschwindigkeitsbeschränk-ung (-en) | speed limit |
| das Tempolimit (-s) | speed limit |
| überschreiten (er überschreitet) (s; insep) | to break, exceed |
| das Bußgeld | fine |
| 50 DM zahlen | to pay 50 DM |
| Gas geben (er gibt) (s) | to accelerate |
| langsamer fahren* | to slow down |
| überholen (insep) | to overtake |
| an (+Dat) ... vorbeifahren (s; sep) | to drive past |
| gesperrt | closed, blocked |
| die Straße ist wieder frei | the road is open again |

| | |
|---|---|
| die Bundesstraße (-n) | A-road, maintained by central Government |
| die Landstraße (-n) | B-road, country road |
| die Spur (-en) | lane |
| die Fahrbahn (-en) | carriageway |
| die Schnellstraße (-n) | dual carriageway |
| die Zufahrt (-en) | approach road |
| bitte einordnen | get in lane |
| die Autobahn (-en) | motorway |
| die Einfahrt (-en) | access road, sliproad |
| die Ausfahrt (-en) | exit road |
| das Autobahnkreuz (-e) | 2 motorways crossing |
| das Autobahndreieck (-e) | 2 motorways merging |
| der Kreisverkehr | roundabout |
| der Rastplatz (⁻e) | motorway lay-by/picnic area |
| die Raststätte (-n) ⎫ der Rasthof (⁻e) ⎬ | motorway service area |
| der Seitenstreifen (-) | hard shoulder |

| | |
|---|---|
| die Gefahr (-en) | danger |
| gefährlich | dangerous |
| passieren* ⎫ geschehen* (es geschieht) (s) ⎬ | to happen |
| der Unfall (⁻e) | accident |
| überfahren (er überfährt) (s; insep) | to run over |
| der Zusammenstoß (⁻e) | collision |
| der Zeuge (-n, -n) ⎫ die Zeugin (-nen) ⎬ | witness (m/f) |
| die Panne (-n) | breakdown |
| der Notruf (-e) | emergency call |
| abschleppen (sep) | to tow away |
| der Abschleppwagen (-) | breakdown vehicle |
| verletzt | injured |
| umkommen* (s; sep) ⎫ ums Leben kommen* (er kommt ums Leben) (s) ⎬ | to die (in an accident) |

| | |
|---|---|
| der ADAC, der AvD | German motoring organisations |
| die Versicherung (-en) | insurance |
| die grüne (Versicherungs)Karte | Green Card (insurance) |
| die Steuermarke (-n) | tax disc |

|  |  |
|---|---|
| **trampen** | to hitchhike |
| **der Tramper (-)** ⎫ | |
| **die Tramperin (-nen)** ⎭ | hitchhiker (*m/f*) |
| **per Anhalter fahren\* (er fährt) (*s*)** | to hitchhike |
| **mitfahren\* (er fährt mit) (*s; sep*)** | to get a lift |

 For car repair vocabulary see Breakdown, page 149.

---

## Jetzt bist du dran! 45

*Was bedeuten diese* *Straßenschilder?*
*What do these traffic signs mean?*

1 *Vor mir steht eine _ _ _ _ _.*

2 *Vorsicht! Vor uns sind _ _ _ _ _ _ _ _ _ _ _ _ _ _ _ _ _.*

3 *über uns sind _ _ _ _ _ _ _ _ _ _. Wir sind in der Nähe eines _ _ _ _ _ _ _ _ s.*

4 *Wir dürfen hier nicht über 60*
*_ _ _ _ _ _ _ _ _ _ _ _ _ _ _ _ _ _ _ _.*

5 *Auf dieser Straße dürfen Fahrzeuge nur in eine _ _ _ _ _ _ _ _ fahren.*

6 *Kein Lkw darf ein Auto _ _ _ _ _ _ _ _ _.*

7 *Auf dieser Straße sind oft _ _ _ _ _ _ _: wir sind vielleicht in der Nähe einer _ _ _ _ _ _.*

8 *Vorsicht! Vor uns fährt vielleicht ein _ _ _ über die Straße!*

9 *Wir müssen vorsichtig fahren. Da ist ein*
*_ _ _ _ _ _ _ _ _ _ _ _ _.*

10 *Man darf hier nicht _ _ _ _ _ _ _.*

---

### d Die Tankstelle — The service station

| | |
|---|---|
| die Autowäsche (-n) | car-wash |
| die Tankstelle (-n) | petrol/service station |
| tanken | to buy petrol |
| volltanken (*sep*) | to fill up (*the petrol tank*) |
| die Selbstbedienung | self-service |
| die SB-Tankstelle (-n) | self-service petrol station |
| die Zapfsäule (-n) | petrol pump |
| das Benzin | petrol, also 2-star petrol |
| Normal | regular/2-star petrol |
| das Super | 4-star |
| für 50 Mark Super | 50 Marks' worth of 4-star |
| verbleit | leaded |
| bleifrei | unleaded |
| der Diesel | diesel (*fuel*) |
| das Öl | oil |
| der Ölwechsel (-) | oil change |

### e Die Panne — Breakdown

| | |
|---|---|
| der Mechaniker (-) }<br>die Mechanikerin (-nen) } | mechanic (*m/f*) |
| die Reparaturwerkstatt (¨-en) | repair garage |
| der Dienst (-e) | service |
| sein Auto wird gewartet | his car is being serviced |
| reparieren | to repair |
| die Reparatur (-en) | repair |
| kaputt | broken |
| abschleppen (*sep*) | to tow away |
| der Abschleppwagen (-) | tow-truck |

| | |
|---|---|
| der Tank ist leer | we've run out of petrol |
| heißgelaufen | overheated |
| das Ersatzrad (¨-er) | spare wheel |
| der Wagenheber (-) | jack |
| der Reifen (-) | tyre |
| die Reifenpanne (-n) | puncture |
| prüfen | to check |
| nachsehen (er sieht nach)<br>(s; *sep*) | to check up (*transitive &<br>intransitive*) |
| der Luftdruck/Reifendruck | tyre pressure |
| aufpumpen (*sep*) | to pump up |

## f Der Bus und die Straßenbahn — The bus and tram

|  |  |
|---|---|
| der Bus/Autobus (-se) | bus |
| der Reisebus (-se) | coach |
| der Doppeldeckerbus (-se) | double-decker bus |
| die Straßenbahn (-en) | tram |
| der Straßenbahnwagen (-) | tramcar |

|  |  |
|---|---|
| der Einstieg (-e) | entrance |
| der Ausstieg (-e) | exit |
| die Haltestelle (-n) | bus/tram-stop |
| der Busbahnhof (¨e) | bus station |
| die Endstation (-en) | terminus, end of the route |
| die Linie (-n) | route |
| der Fahrschein (-e) <br> die Fahrkarte (-n) | ticket |
| der Busfahrer <br> Straßenbahnfahrer (-) | bus/tram driver |
| der Schaffner (-) <br> die Schaffnerin (-nen) | conductor (*m/f*) |
| die Zeitkarte (-n) | season ticket |
| die Mehrfahrtenkarte (-n) | ticket valid for several journeys |
| (un)gültig | (in)valid |
| der Fahrscheinautomat (-en, -en) | ticket machine |
| schwarzfahren (er fährt schwarz) (*s; sep*) | to travel without paying |
| der Schwarzfahrer (-) | fare-dodger |
| Sie fahren mit der Zwölf | you take the no 12 |
| halten (er hält) (*s*) | to stop |
| festhalten (er hält fest) (*s; sep*) | to hold tight |

## g Die Bahn — The railway

|  |  |
|---|---|
| der Bahnhof (¨e) | railway station |
| der Hauptbahnhof (¨e) (Hbf) | main station |
| die U-Bahnstation (-en) | underground station |
| die Unterführung (-en) | subway |
| das Gleis (-e) | platform, track |
| der Bahnsteig (-e) | (*built up*) platform |
| die (Eisen)bahn | railway |
| das Eisen | iron |
| der Stahl | steel |
| die Deutsche Bahn (DB) | German railways |

| die U-Bahn | underground, tube |
| die S-Bahn | suburban railway |
| der Zug (¨e) | train |
| der Intercity/IC-Zug | inter-city train |
| der D-Zug (¨e) | express, through train |
| der Eilzug (¨e) | fast stopping-train |
| der Schnellzug (¨e) | express, fast train |
| der Nahverkehrszug | local train |
| der Nahverkehr | local journeys |
| die Lokomotive (-n)/die Lok (-s) | locomotive, engine |
| der Lokführer (-) | engine driver |
| die Dampflok (-s) | steam locomotive |
| die Diesellok (-s) | diesel locomotive |
| die Elektrolok (-s) | electric locomotive |
| der Wagen (-) | coach, carriage |
| der Wagen erster Klasse | first class carriage |
| der Speisewagen (-) | dining car, buffet car |
| der Schlafwagen (-) | sleeping-car |
| der Liegewagen (-) | couchette coach |
| der Liegeplatz (¨e) | couchette |
| das Abteil (-e) | compartment |
| der Platz (¨e) | seat |
| der Raucherplatz / Nichtraucherplatz (¨e) | (no-)smoking seat |
| frei | free, unoccupied |
| besetzt | occupied |
| das Gepäcknetz (-e) | luggage rack |
| der Gang (¨e) | corridor |
| der Zug verkehrt regelmäßig | the train runs regularly |
| abfahren* (er fährt ... ab) (s; sep) | to depart |
| die Abfahrt (-en) | departure |
| ankommen* (er kommt ... an) (s; sep) | to arrive |
| die Ankunft (¨e) | arrival |
| halten (er hält) (s) | to stop |
| pünktlich | punctual(ly) |
| um 5 Minuten verspätet | 5 minutes late |
| eine Verspätung von 5 Minuten | a 5-minute delay |
| planmäßig | as scheduled |
| der Fahrplan (¨e) | timetable |
| anschauen (sep) | to look at |
| blicken auf (+Acc) | to glance at |

| | |
|---|---|
| werktags/wochentags | on working-days (*Mon–Sat*) |
| einsteigen* in (er steigt ein) (*s; sep*) | to get in |
| umsteigen* (*s; sep*) | to change |
| aussteigen* aus (*s; sep*) | to get out |
| zusteigen* (*s; sep*) | to join the train |
| direkt | directly, without changing |
| dieser Zug fährt durch nach München | this train goes to Munich without changing |
| die Verbindung (-en) | connection |
| noch jemand zugestiegen? | Any more fares, please? |
| der Zuschlag (¨e) | supplement (on fare) |
| zuschlagpflichtig | subject to supplementary charge |
| die Gebühr (-en) | fee, charge |
| gebührenpflichtig | chargeable |
| erreichen (*insep*) | to catch |
| verpassen (*insep*) | to miss |
| sich hinauslehnen (*sep*) | to lean out |
| bitte nicht hinauslehnen | please do not lean out of the window |
| ab Aachen (*Dat*) | from Aachen onwards |
| die Fahrkarte (-n) | ticket |
| der Fahrschein (-e) <br> der Fahrausweis (-e) } | ticket (*formal words*) |
| der Schalter/Fahrkartenschalter (-) | ticket office |
| der Fahrpreis (-e) | fare |
| die Ermäßigung (-en) | reduction |
| ermäßigt | reduced |
| die Monatskarte <br> Wochenkarte (-n) } | monthly/weekly season |
| die einfache Fahrkarte | single ticket |
| die Rückfahrkarte (-n) | return ticket |
| einmal nach Bonn hin und zurück | one return to Bonn |
| zweimal einfach nach Köln | two singles to Cologne |
| einmal erste Klasse einfach nach Kiel | a first class single to Kiel |
| lösen | to buy (*a ticket*) |
| entwerten (*insep*) | to stamp (*a ticket*) |
| der Entwerter (-) | stamping machine |
| kontrollieren | to check |
| der Schaffner (-) | ticket collector |
| der Fahrgast (¨e) <br> der Passagier (-e) } | passenger |

| | |
|---|---|
| der Wartesaal (-säle) | waiting room |
| die Auskunft (¨e) ⎫<br>die Information (-en) ⎭ | information |
| können Sie mir sagen...? | can you tell me...? |
| erklären | to explain |
| können Sie mir Bescheid sagen? | can you let me know? |
| der Zeitungskiosk (-e) | newspaper kiosk |
| der Schnellimbiß (-sse) | snack-bar |
| die Imbißhalle (-n) ⎫<br>die Imbißstube (-n) ⎭ | café, cafeteria |
| der Kofferkuli (-s) | luggage trolley |
| das Schließfach (¨er) | luggage locker |
| die Gepäckaufbewahrung | left luggage office |
| das Gepäck aufgeben<br>(er gibt ... auf) (*s; sep*) | to give in one's luggage |
| die Gepäckannahme(stelle) | checking-in counter of left luggage office |
| die Gepäckausgabe(stelle) | checking-out counter of left luggage office |
| versichern (*insep*) | to insure |

## h Die Schiffahrt

## Travel by boat

| | |
|---|---|
| der Hafen (¨) | harbour |
| der Kai (-s) | quay, waterfront |
| die Landungsbrücke (-n) | landing stage, jetty |
| das Schiff (-e) | boat, ship |
| der Dampfer (-) | steamer |
| die Fähre (-n) | ferry |
| die Autofähre (-n) | car ferry |
| an Bord gehen* (*s*) | to board |
| an Deck gehen* (*s*) | to go up on deck |
| das Boot (-e) | (small) boat |
| segeln | to sail |
| das Segelboot (-e) | sailing boat |
| das Ruderboot (-e) | rowing boat |
| rudern | to row |
| das Motorboot (-e) | motor boat |
| das Luftkissenfahrzeug (-e) | hovercraft |
| das Tragflügelboot (-e) | jetfoil |
| die Kreuzfahrt (-en) | cruise |
| die Überfahrt (-en) | crossing |
| die Hafenrundfahrt (-en) | trip round the harbour |
| seekrank | sea-sick |

| | |
|---|---|
| der Ärmelkanal | English Channel |
| die Nordsee | North Sea |
| die Ostsee | Baltic Sea |

### i Der Luftverkehr — Air traffic

| | |
|---|---|
| die Luft | air |
| das Flugzeug (-e) | aeroplane |
| das Charterflugzeug (-e) | charter plane |
| der Jumbo-Jet (-s) | jumbo jet |
| die Maschine (-n) | aircraft |
| die Boeing | Boeing (*all makes of plane are feminine*) |
| der Hubschrauber (-) | helicopter |
| der Flughafen (÷) | airport |
| das (Flug)ticket (-s) } die Flugkarte (-n) } | ticket |
| der Fluggast (÷e) | passenger |
| der Warteraum (÷e) | lounge |
| einchecken (*sep*) | to check in |
| starten* | to start |
| nach ... abfliegen* (er fliegt ... ab) (*s; sep*) | to take off for... |
| der Abflug (÷e) | take-off |
| fliegen* (er fliegt) (*s*) | to fly |
| der Flug (÷e) | flight |
| in einer Flughöhe von 10 000 Metern | at 10,000 metres' altitude |
| landen* | to land |
| die Landung (-en) | landing |
| eine Zwischenlandung machen | to make a stop-over |
| der Steward (-s) | steward |
| die Stewardeß (-ssen) | stewardess |

### j Probleme — Problems

| | |
|---|---|
| das Problem (-e) | problem |
| der Stau (-e *or* -s) } die Verkehrsstauung (-en) } | traffic-jam |
| der Sturm (÷e) } das Unwetter } | gale, storm |
| das Gewitter | thunder storm |
| reisekrank/seekrank | travel-sick/sea-sick |

| | |
|---|---|
| die Reisekrankheit | travel-sickness |
| sich erholen (*insep*) | to recover |
| in den falschen Zug steigen* (er steigt) (*s*) | to board the wrong train |
| in die falsche Richtung schicken | to send in the wrong direction |
| den Anschluß verpassen (*insep*) | to miss one's connection |
| die Verspätung (-en) | delay |
| um eine Stunde verspätet | delayed by one hour |
| die Panne (-n) | breakdown |
| ausfallen (er fällt aus) (*s; sep*) | to be cancelled (*of train*) |
| der Streik (-s) | strike |
| streiken | to strike |
| sich verfahren (er verfährt sich) (*s; insep*) | to get lost (*driving*) |
| das Gepäck verlieren (er verliert) (*s; insep*) | to lose one's luggage |

## Jetzt bist du dran! 46

*Was denkst du über Autos, Busse, usw? Bilde Sätze!*

*What do you think about cars, buses, etc? Make up sentences.*

Beispiel: *Das Beste am InterCity Zug ist, daß er so schnell ist.*

| | | | |
|---|---|---|---|
| Das Gute | am Bus | ist, daß er | so ruhig/laut ist |
| Das Beste | am Auto | ist, daß sie | so schnell/langsam ist |
| Das Schöne | an der Autobahn | ist, daß es | so billig/teuer ist |
| Das Schlechte | am Taxi | ist, daß man | so interessant/langweilig ist |
| | an der U-Bahn | | allein/mit Freunden fahren kann. |
| | am InterCity Zug | | dabei lesen kann. |
| | am Flugzeug | | immer/nie einen Halt machen kann. |
| | am Fahrrad | | (nicht) im Freien ist. |
| | am Motorrad | | manchmal/nie im Stau ist. |
| | am Luftkissenfahrzeug | | reisekrank sein kann. |
| | am Schiff | | viel/nichts sieht. |

**Jetzt bist du dran! 47**

| Welche Wörter gehören zusammen? | Which words belong together? |
|---|---|

| | |
|---|---|
| die Panne | das Flugticket |
| die Gepäckannahme | die Abfahrt |
| die Kontrolle | der Sicherheitsgurt |
| das Gleis | die Auskunft |
| einchecken | die Zapfsäule |
| Straßenarbeiten | sich hinsetzen |
| der Sturm | der Koffer |
| abfliegen | die Verspätung |
| sich anschnallen | die Geschwindigkeitsbeschränkung |
| die Tankstelle | der Schaffner |
| der Fahrplan | die Seekrankheit |
| einsteigen | landen |

# D:The world of work

## 1 Arbeit und Studium — Work and study

### a Der Schulabgang — Leaving school

| | |
|---|---|
| die Schule verlassen (er verläßt) (*s; insep*) | to leave school |
| (un)gern | (un)willingly |
| eine Stelle suchen | to look for a job |
| sich um eine Stelle bewerben (er bewirbt) (*s; insep*) | to apply for a job |
| die Bewerbung (-en) | application |
| das Antragsformular (-e) | application form |
| Arbeit finden (als...) (er findet) (*s*) | to find employment (as...) |
| der Lehrgang (-̈e) | training-course, apprenticeship |
| das Arbeitspraktikum | work experience |
| der/die Azubi (-s) | trainee (*m/f*) |
| der Praktikant (-en, -en) | trainee (*m*) |
| die Praktikantin (-nen) | trainee (*f*) |
| arbeitslos | unemployed |
| beschäftigt | employed/busy |
| der Student (-en, -en) ⎫ die Studentin (-nen) ⎭ | student (*m/f; at college/ university*) |
| studieren | to study (at college/university) |
| zur Universität gehen* (*s*) | to go to university |
| auf/an der Universität sein* (*s*) | to be at university |
| die Universität besuchen | to go to a university |
| auf/an der Universität Nottingham | at Nottingham University |

### b Studienkurse — Courses of study

| | |
|---|---|
| der Kurs (-e) | course |
| das Studium (Studien) | study |
| weiterstudieren (*sep*) | to continue one's studies |
| der Studienplatz (-̈e) | place at university |
| die Universität (-en)/die Uni (-s) | university |
| die Hochschule (-n) | college, university |
| die Berufsschule (-n) | vocational school |
| die Fachhochschule (-n) | special technical college |
| die Fachschule (-) | technical college |
| die kaufmännische Fachschule (-n) | business school |

| | |
|---|---|
| die Handelsschule (-n) | commercial college |
| die pädagogische Hochschule | teacher-training college |
| die technische Hochschule | technical college/university |
| die Volkshochschule | adult education centre |

| | |
|---|---|
| einen akademischen Grad erhalten (er erhält) (s) | to get a degree |
| das Diplom (-e) | diploma |
| ich möchte ein Diplom machen | I'd like to take a diploma |
| das Staatsexamen machen | to take a degree (*the exams*) |
| promovieren | to take a doctorate |
| die Forschung (-en) | research |
| ich kriege BAFöG | I get a grant |
| das Darlehen (-) | loan |

| | |
|---|---|
| (die) Geisteswissenschaften (*pl*) | the Arts |
| (die) Naturwissenschaften (*pl*) | the Sciences |
| (die) Medizin | Medicine |
| Jura | Law |
| (die) Germanistik | German studies |
| (die) Romanistik | Romance languages/French studies |
| (die) Anglistik | English studies |
| (die) Wirtschaftswissenschaften (*pl*) | Economics |

 See also Timetable, for more subjects, pages 27–8.

## c Zunkunftspläne — Future plans

| | |
|---|---|
| die Zukunft | future |
| der Plan (¨e) | plan |
| vorhaben (er hat vor) (*sep*) | to intend |
| die Absicht (-en) | intention |
| das Ziel (-e) | goal |
| der Berufswunsch (¨e) | desired job |
| die Berufsberatung | careers advice |
| die Oberstufe | sixth form |
| das Duale System | system of school attendance & apprenticeship |
| die Ausbildung | training |
| die Lehre (-n) | apprenticeship, training |
| der Lehrling (-e) } der/die Auszubildende (*adj. noun*) } | apprentice/trainee |
| ich möchte eine Lehre machen | I'd like to do an apprenticeship |

| | |
|---|---|
| ein soziales Jahr | a gap-year |
| zum Militär gehen* (s) | to join the armed forces |
| der Militärdienst | military service |
| der Zivildienst | community service (*alternative to military service*) |

| | |
|---|---|
| ich möchte Arzt werden | I'd like to become a doctor |
| ich denke daran, Arzt zu werden | I'm thinking of becoming a doctor |
| selbständig | independent/self-employed |
| der menschliche Kontakt | human contact |
| helfen (+Dat) (er hilft) (s) | to help |
| heiraten | to marry |
| eine Familie gründen | to start a family |
| nach ... umziehen* (er zieht ... um) (s; sep) | to move to... |

## d Der Arbeitsmarkt — The job market

| | |
|---|---|
| die Teilzeitarbeit ⎫ die Halbtagsarbeit ⎬ | part-time work/job |
| die Ganztagsstelle (-n) | full-time job |
| die Dauerbeschäftigung (-en) | permanent position |
| als Aushilfe arbeiten | to temp |
| der Job (-s) | temporary job |
| die Saisonarbeit | seasonal work |

| | |
|---|---|
| Erfahrung haben | to have experience |
| der Lebenslauf (-̈e) | CV |
| das Vorstellungsgespräch (-e) | interview |
| sich bewerben um (+Acc) (er bewirbt sich um...) (s; insep) | to apply for |
| die Konkurrenz | competition |
| die Qualifikation (-en) | qualification (*on paper*) |
| die Voraussetzung (en) | qualification, requirement |
| gebildet sein* | to be informed, educated |

| | |
|---|---|
| arbeiten | to work |
| der Arbeiter (-) | worker (*m*) |
| die Arbeiterin (-nen) | worker (*f*) |
| der Arbeitgeber (-) | employer |
| der Arbeitnehmer (-) ⎫ die Arbeitnehmerin (-nen) ⎬ | employee (*m/f*) |
| das Arbeitsamt | job centre |

| arbeitslos | unemployed |
|---|---|
| die Stelle (-n) | job, position |
| die Arbeitsstelle (-n) | job |
| der Beruf (-e) | profession |
| berufstätig | employed, having a job |

| einstellen (*sep*) | to take on (*employees*) |
|---|---|
| die Einstellung | recruitment |
| wenn möglich | if possible |
| vielleicht | perhaps |
| eventuell | possibly |
| wahrscheinlich | probably |

## e Berufe       Jobs

| *male* | *female* | *job* |
|---|---|---|
| der Apotheker (-) | die Apothekerin (-nen) | chemist, pharmacist |
| der Arzt (¨-e) | die Ärztin (-nen) | doctor |
| der Tierarzt (¨-e) | die Tierärztin (-nen) | vet |
| der Zahnarzt (¨-e) | die Zahnärztin (-nen) | dentist |
| der Bäcker (-) | die Bäckerin (-nen) | baker |
| der Bauarbeiter (-) | die Bauarbeiterin (-nen) | building worker |
| der Bauer (-n, -n) | die Bäuerin (-nen) | farmer |
| der Beamte (*adj. noun in m*) | die Beamtin (-nen) | civil servant, official |
| der Briefträger (-) | die Briefträgerin (-nen) | postman/-woman |
| der Bürgermeister (-) | die Bürgermeisterin (-nen) | mayor |
| der/die Büroangestellte (*adj. noun*) | | white-collar worker |
| der Busfahrer (-) | die Busfahrerin (-nen) | bus-driver |
| der Chef (-s) | die Chefin (-nen) | boss |
| der Direktor (-en) | die Direktorin (-nen) | director |
| der Dolmetscher (-) | die Dolmetscherin (-nen) | interpreter |
| der Drogist (-en, -en) | die Drogistin (-nen) | chemist (*not dispensing*) |
| der Elektriker (-) | die Elektrikerin (-nen) | electrician |
| der Fabrikarbeiter (-) | die Fabrikarbeiterin (-nen) | factory worker |
| der Fahrer (-) | die Fahrerin (-nen) | driver |
| der Feuerwehrmann (¨-er) | | fireman |
| der Fleischer (-) | die Fleischerin (-nen) } | butcher |
| der Metzger (-) | die Metzgerin (-nen) } | |
| der Friseur (-e) | die Friseurin (-nen) | hairdresser |
| der Fußballspieler (-) | die Fußballspielerin (-nen) | footballer |
| der Geschäftsmann (-leute) | die Geschäftsfrau (-en) | businessman/-woman |
| der Hausmann (¨-er) | die Hausfrau (-en) | househusband/-wife |
| der Ingenieur (-e) | die Ingenieurin (-nen) | engineer |
| der Journalist (-en, -en) | die Journalistin (-nen) | journalist |
| der Kassierer (-) | die Kassiererin (-nen) | cashier, bank-clerk |

| | | |
|---|---|---|
| der Kaufmann (-leute) | die Kauffrau (-en) | businessman/-woman |
| der Kellner (-) | die Kellnerin (-nen) | waiter/waitress |
| der Klempner (-) | die Klempnerin (-nen) | plumber |
| der Koch (¨e) | die Köchin (-nen) | chef, cook |
| der Kollege (-n, -n) | die Kollegin (-nen) | colleague |
| der Krankenpfleger (-) | die Krankenschwester (-n) | nurse |
| der Lehrer (-) | die Lehrerin (-nen) | teacher |
| der Lkw-Fahrer (-) | die Lkw-Fahrerin (-nen) | lorry-driver |
| der Manager (-) | die Managerin (-nen) | manager |
| der Matrose (-n, -n) | | sailor |
| der Mechaniker (-) | die Mechanikerin (-nen) | mechanic |
| der Musiker (-) | die Musikerin (-nen) | musician |
| der Pfarrer (-) | die Pfarrerin (-) | vicar (*Protestant*) |
| der Pilot (-en, -en) | die Pilotin (-nen) | pilot |
| der Polizist (-en, -en) | die Polizistin (-nen) | policeman/policewoman |
| der Priester (-) | | priest (*Roman Catholic*) |
| der Putzmann (¨er) | die Putzfrau (-en) | cleaner |
| der Rechtsanwalt (¨e) | die Rechtsanwältin (-nen) | lawyer |
| der Rentner (-) | die Rentnerin (-nen) | retired person, senior citizen |
| der Reporter (-) | die Reporterin (-nen) | reporter |
| der Schaffner (-) | die Schaffnerin (-nen) | (*bus*) conductor, ticket collector |
| der Schauspieler (-) | die Schauspielerin (-nen) | actor/actress |
| der Schiedsrichter (-) | die Schiedsrichterin (-nen) | referee |
| der Schreibwaren-händler (-) | die Schreibwaren-händlerin (-nen) | stationer |
| der Sekretär (-e) | die Sekretärin (-nen) | secretary |
| der Soldat (-en, -en) | die Soldatin (-nen) | soldier |
| der Sozialarbeiter (-) | die Sozialarbeiterin (-nen) | social worker |
| der Steward (-s) | die Stewardeß (-essen) | air steward(ess) |
| der Verkäufer (-) | die Verkäuferin (-nen) | salesman/saleswoman |
| | das Zimmermädchen (-) | chambermaid |

| | |
|---|---|
| babysitten | to babysit |
| beim Bau/auf dem Bau arbeiten | to be a building worker |
| bei der Bahn arbeiten | to work on the railways |
| in Rente gehen* (s) | to retire |

| | |
|---|---|
| der Betrieb (-e) | business, factory |
| die Firma (Firmen) | firm |
| die Industrie (-n) | industry |
| das Werk (-e) | factory, plant |
| die Fabrik (-en) | factory |
| das Labor (-s) | lab |
| das Büro (-s) | office |

| | |
|---|---|
| **tippen** | to type |
| **ablegen** (*sep*) | to file (away) |
| **die Besprechung** (-en) | meeting |
| **die Konferenz** (-en) | conference, meeting |
| **die Arbeitsbedingungen** (*pl*) | working conditions |
| **feste Arbeitszeit** | fixed hours |
| **gleitende Arbeitszeit** | flexible hours |
| **regelmäßige Arbeitszeit** | regular hours |
| **die Überstunden** (*pl*) | overtime |
| **die Schichtarbeit** | shift work |
| **am Fließband arbeiten** | to work at the conveyor belt |

## Jetzt bist du dran! 48

*Was sind diese Berufe?*          *What are these jobs?*

1   Er bringt die Post.                    der _ _ _ _ _ _ _ _ _ _ _

2   Im Restaurant bringt sie,           die _ _ _ _ _ _ _ _ _
     was wir bestellt haben.

3   Er nimmt unser Geld in der        der _ _ _ _ _ _ _ _
     Straßenbahn.

4   Sie macht uns das Haar schön. die _ _ _ _ _ _ _ _ _

5   Er ist auf dem Fußballfeld aber   der _ _ _ _ _ _ _ _ _ _ _ _ _
     spielt nicht.

6   Sie arbeitet im Flugzeug.      die _ _ _ _ _ _ _ _ _

7   Er macht die Stadt               der _ _ _ _ _ _ _ _
     sicher, hoffentlich!

8   Sie unterrichtet.                    die _ _ _ _ _ _ _ _

9   Er bereitet das Essen in einem    der _ _ _ _
     Restaurant vor.

10  Sie spielt vielleicht Geige oder    die _ _ _ _ _ _ _ _ _
     Flöte.

| | |
|---|---|
| **f Arbeitslosigkeit** | **Unemployment** |
| **arbeitslos** | unemployed |
| **der/die Arbeitslose** (*adj. noun*) | unemployed person |
| **der/die Arbeitsuchende** (*adj. noun*) | person looking for work |
| **Arbeit suchen** | to look for work |
| **den Arbeitsplatz verlieren** | to be made redundant |
| **entlassen** (*s; insep*) | to sack |
| **vorzeitig in den Ruhestand gehen*** | to take early retirement |
| **der Streik** (-s) | strike |
| **die Gewerkschaft** (-en) | trade union |
| **das Arbeitsamt** (-̈er) | job centre |
| **sich anmelden** (*sep*) | to register |
| **Arbeitslosengeld beziehen** (**er bezieht**) (*s; insep*) | to draw unemployment benefit |
| **die Kleinanzeige** (-n) | small ad |
| **die Stellenanzeige** (-n) | job advert |

| | |
|---|---|
| **g Die Finanzen** | **Finances** |
| **das Gehalt** (-̈er) | salary |
| **der Lohn** (-̈e) | wages |
| **verdienen** (*insep*) | to earn |
| **gut verdienen** (*insep*) | to earn good money |
| **...pro Stunde/Woche verdienen** | to earn ... per hour/week |
| **die Lohnerhöhung** (-en) | pay rise |
| **reich** | rich |
| **ein Vermögen machen** | to make a fortune |
| **arm** | poor |
| **die Armut** | poverty |
| **pleite gehen** | to go broke |
| **die Lebenserhaltungskosten** (*pl*) | cost of living |
| **sparen** | to save up |
| **sich** (*Dat*) **leisten können** | to be able to afford |
| **leihen** (*s*) | to lend/borrow |
| **borgen** | to borrow |
| **kaufen** | to buy |
| **verkaufen** | to sell |
| **Geld ausgeben** (*s*) | to spend money |

## Jetzt bist du dran! 49

*Ergänze die Sätze!*  Complete the sentences.

1  Jemand, der ganz viel Geld hat, ist _ _ _ _ _.

2  Das Amt, wo man hoffentlich Arbeit findet, ist das
   _ _ _ _ _ _ _ _ _ _.

3  Man kann eine Fabrik auch einen _ _ _ _ _ _ _ nennen.

4  Das Geld, das man für seine Arbeit bekommt, ist das _ _ _ _ _ _
   oder der _ _ _ _.

5  Jemand, der mit dir arbeitet, ist ein _ _ _ _ _ _ _ oder eine
   _ _ _ _ _ _ _ _.

6  Jemand, der viel Geld für seine Arbeit bekommt, _ _ _ _ _ _ _ _ _ gut.

7  Ein anderes Wort für eine Managerin ist eine _ _ _ _ _ _.

8  Jemand, der in einer Fabrik arbeitet, ist natürlich ein
   _ _ _ _ _ _ _ _ _ _ _ _ _.

9  Wenn eine Fabrik mehr produzieren will, muß sie mehr Leute
   _ _ _ _ _ _ _ _ _ _.

10  Jemand, der Arbeit hat, ist _ _ _ _ _ _ _ _ _ _ _.

## 2 Kommunikationen     Communications

### a Begrüßungen     Greetings

| | |
|---|---|
| herein! | come in! |
| hallo! | hallo! |
| servus! (*S Germany & Austria*) | hallo/goodbye |
| der Gruß (⸚e) | greeting |
| grüßen | to say hallo, greet |

| | |
|---|---|
| grüß Gott! (*S Germany & Austria*) <br> grüß dich! } | hallo! |
| prost!/zum Wohl! | cheers! |
| sich verabschieden (*insep*) | to say goodbye |
| alles Gute! <br> mach's gut! } | all the best! |
| auf Wiedersehen! | goodbye! |
| tschüs! | goodbye! (*informal*) |
| komm gut nach Hause! | safe journey home! |
| bis gleich! | see you in a moment! |
| bis morgen! | see you tomorrow! |

## b Das Gespräch — Conversation

| | |
|---|---|
| duzen | to call someone *du* |
| siezen | to call someone *Sie* |
| sagen | to say, tell |
| sprechen (er spricht) (*s*) | to speak |
| stimmen | to be right (*of a fact*) |
| recht haben | to be right (*of a person*) |
| unrecht haben | to be wrong (*of a person*) |
| Sie haben recht/unrecht | you are right/wrong |
| es war mir ein Vergnügen | it was a pleasure |
| das macht nichts | it doesn't matter |
| das ist nicht schlimm | don't worry |
| denken an (+ *Acc*) (er denkt) (*irreg w*) | to think of |
| glauben (+*Dat*) | to believe (a person) |
| meinen | to think, say |
| was meinst du? | what do you think? |
| einverstanden | agreed/in agreement |
| wirklich? | really? |
| ach (so)! | oh, really! |

## c Probleme im Gespräch — Problems in conversation

| | |
|---|---|
| verstehen (er versteht) (*s; insep*) | to understand |
| das Mißverständnis (-se) | misunderstanding |
| kapieren | to understand (*colloquial*) |
| das Wort (-e *or* ¨er) | word |
| das Wörterbuch (¨er) | dictionary |
| übersetzen (*insep*) | to translate |
| sich entschuldigen (*insep*) | to apologise |
| Entschuldigung! <br> Verzeihung! } | excuse me!, sorry! |

| | |
|---|---|
| verzeihen (+*Dat*) (s) (er verzeiht) | to excuse, pardon |
| wie, bitte? | pardon? |
| wieso? | how come? |
| Augenblick mal!/Moment mal! | just a moment! |
| leise | soft(ly) |
| können Sie lauter sprechen? | can you speak more loudly? |
| deutlich | clear(ly) |
| wiederholen (*insep*) | to repeat |
| aussprechen (er spricht ... aus) (*s; sep*) | to pronounce |
| bedeuten (*insep*) | to mean |
| das Gegenteil | opposite |
| gewiß | certain(ly) |
| die Idee (-n) | idea |
| das ist eine gute Idee | that's a good idea |
| ich habe keine Ahnung | I have no idea |
| nicht wahr? | isn't it, won't we? |
| Pech haben | to be unlucky |
| der Quatsch/der Unsinn | rubbish, nonsense |
| wissen (*irreg w*) | to know (*a fact*) |
| natürlich | of course |
| bestimmt | definitely |
| eben! | precisely! |
| abgemacht! | agreed! |
| nachdenken (er denkt ... nach) (*irreg w; sep*) | to ponder, think |
| sich fragen | to wonder |
| verbessern (*insep*) | to improve (*transitive*) |

## d Briefe — Letters

| | |
|---|---|
| der Brief (-e) | letter |
| schreiben (er schreibt) (s) | to write |
| schicken | to send |
| abschicken (*sep*) | to post, send off |
| der Absender (-) (Abs.) | sender |
| einwerfen (er wirft ... ein) (*s; sep*) | to post (*in letter-box*) |
| beilegen (*sep*) | to enclose (*in a letter*) |
| einen Brief per Einschreiben schicken | to register a letter |
| Lieber/-e X | Dear X (*informal*) |
| Sehr geehrter Herr (usw) | Dear Sir |

| | |
|---|---|
| Sehr geehrte Damen und Herren | Dear Sir or Madam |
| der Gruß (Grüße) | greeting |
| Grüße bestellen (*insep*) (*an +Acc*) | to send best wishes to |
| ich danke Ihnen im voraus | thank you in advance |
| Schluß machen | to finish off |
| (ich bestelle) Grüße an Deine Eltern | (I send) my regards to your parents |
| mit freundlichem/bestem Gruß mit freundlichen/besten Grüßen } | with best wishes, yours |
| hochachtungsvoll | yours faithfully |

 See also The post office, pages 141–2.

## e Am Telephon    Telephoning

| | |
|---|---|
| niemand meldet sich | no one's answering |
| besetzt | engaged |
| das Gespräch (-e) | conversation/call |
| die Verbindung (-en) | connection |
| verbinden (er verbindet) (s; insep) | to connect |
| sie sind falsch verbunden | you've got the wrong number |
| die falsche Nummer | wrong number |
| der Anschluß | telephone connection |
| | |
| hallo! | hallo! |
| wer ist da? | who's there? |
| hier bei Ross | this is the Rosses' house |
| hier Michael Ross | Michael Ross here |
| kann ich bitte Herrn Ross sprechen? | can I speak to Mr Ross, please? |
| am Apparat | speaking |
| bleiben Sie am Apparat! | don't hang up |
| ich verbinde Sie | I'm putting you through |
| möchten Sie eine Nachricht hinterlassen? | would you like to leave a message? |
| kann ich etwas ausrichten? | can I take a message? |
| wie schreibt man das? | how is that spelt? |
| können Sie langsamer sprechen? | can you speak more slowly? |
| können Sie später noch mal anrufen? | can you call back later? |
| auf Wiederhören | good-bye (*on telephone*) |
| | |
| das Telefon (-e) | telephone |
| das Mobiltelefon (-e) | mobile phone |

| der Anrufbeantworter (-) | answer phone |
| der Hörer (-) | receiver |
| abnehmen (er nimmt ... ab) (s; sep) | to pick up |
| auflegen (sep) | to hang up |
| die Telefonnummer (-n) | telephone number |
| das Telefonbuch (¨er) | telephone directory |
| nachschlagen (er schlägt nach) (s; sep) | to look up |
| telefonieren mit (+Dat) | to telephone |
| anrufen (er ruft ... an) (s; sep) | to telephone, ring up |
| der Anruf (-e) | telephone call |
| wählen | to dial |
| durchwählen (sep) | to dial direct |
| die Durchwahl | direct number |
| die Vorwahl | dialling code |
| drücken | to press |
| die Taste (-n) | button |
| klingeln/läuten | to ring |

| die Telefonzelle (-n) | telephone box |
| öffentlich | public |
| der Fernsprecher (-) | telephone (official word) |
| die Telefonkarte (-n) | phone-card |
| das Kartentelefon (-e) | card-operated phone |
| das Ferngespräch (-e) | long distance call |
| das Ortsgespräch (-e) | local call |
| das R-Gespräch (-e) (Rückgespräch) | reversed charge call |
| die Fernvermittlungsstelle | exchange |
| die Zentrale | switchboard |
| die Vermittlung | operator |
| Apparat 6238 | extension 6238 |
| per Fax | by fax |
| faxen | to fax |
| elektronische Post/E-mail | E-mail |

## f Computer und Informatik — Computers and IT

| der Computer (-) | computer |
| der PC (-s) | table-top computer |
| der Laptop (-s) | lap-top computer |
| das Netzwerk (-e) | network |
| die Diskette (-n) | floppy/soft disk |

| die Festplatte (-n) | hard disk |
| das Diskettenlaufwerk (-e) | disk drive |
| der Microchip (-s) | micro-chip |
| das Paket (-e) | package |
| die Hardware | hardware |
| die Software | software |

| der Bildschirm (-e) | screen, monitor |
| zeigen | to display |
| das Menü | menu |
| der Cursor | cursor |
| die Tabellenkalkulation | spreadsheet |
| die Datei (-en) | file |
| das Fenster (-) | window |
| der Virus (Viren) | virus |
| die Maus | mouse |
| anklicken (*sep*) | to click on |
| ich klicke das Feld an | I click on the button |
| die Tastatur (-en) | keyboard |
| die Taste (-n) | key |
| auf eine Taste drücken | to press a key |
| tippen | to type |
| kursiv | in italics |
| fett | in bold |
| der Großbuchstabe (-ns, -n) | capital letter |
| die Kapitälchen (*pl*) | small capitals |
| die Leertaste (-n) | space-bar |
| der Tabulator | tab |
| die Textverarbeitung | word-processing |

| booten | to boot up |
| ein Programm laden (er lädt) (*s*) | to load a program |
| programmieren | to program |
| einloggen/einklinken (*sep*) | to log on |
| das Paßwort | password |
| einlesen (er liest … ein) (*s; sep*) <br> hereinladen (er lädet … ein) (*s; sep*) | to down-load |
| speichern | to save |
| die Sicherheitskopie/das Backup | back-up |
| löschen | to delete |
| bearbeiten | to edit |
| ausschneiden und einfügen | to cut and paste |
| zusammenführen (*sep*) | to merge |

| | |
|---|---|
| **ausdrucken** (*sep*) | to print |
| **der Drucker** (-) | printer |
| **beenden** (*insep*) | to exit |
| **das Internet** | internet |
| **das Abenteuerspiel** (-e) | adventure game |
| **der Joystick** (-s) | joystick |

## Jetzt bist du dran! 50

Man kann hier Wörter über die
Informatik finden. Man liest
nach oben oder nach unten,
vorwärts oder rückwärts.
Wenn du über 20 findest, ist das
sehr gut.

Find words about Computers
and IT. They read up or down,
forwards or backwards.
If you can find over 20, you
are doing very well.

| B | I | T | M | A | U | S | V | G | E | V |
|---|---|---|---|---|---|---|---|---|---|---|
| U | P | A | N | N | E | N | I | S | K | E |
| C | O | M | P | U | T | E | R | P | U | R |
| H | L | Z | C | A | S | P | U | I | R | A |
| S | I | T | Z | E | A | P | S | E | S | R |
| T | T | E | F | R | T | I | D | L | I | B |
| A | S | N | Ö | D | A | T | E | N | V | E |
| B | O | O | T | E | N | C | H | I | P | I |
| E | T | T | A | L | P | T | S | E | F | T |
| N | N | R | E | H | C | I | E | P | S | E |
| K | A | P | I | T | Ä | L | C | H | E | N |

# E:The International world

| a Geographie | Geography |
|---|---|
| die Welt | world |
| reisen* | to travel |
| der/die Reisende (*adj. noun*) | traveller |
| fremd | unfamiliar |
| ins Ausland | (going) abroad |
| im Ausland | (being) abroad |
| der Ausländer (-) | foreigner (*m*) |
| die Ausländerin (-nen) | foreigner (*f*) |
| ausländisch | foreign |
| die Nationalität (-en) | nationality |
| die Landkarte (-n) | map |
| der Kontinent (-e) } der Erdteil (-e) } | continent |
| Afrika | Africa |
| Amerika | America |
| Asien | Asia |
| Australien | Australia |
| Europa | Europe |
| der Norden | north |
| der Süden | south |
| der Osten | east |
| der Westen | west |

Nord-, Süd-, Ost-, West- *in compounds*

| | |
|---|---|
| Westeuropa | western Europe |
| Südamerika | South America |
| Südostasien | South East Asia |
| Nordamerika | North America |
| nördlich } südlich } östlich } von westlich } | north } south } east } of west } |
| das Land (¨er) | country |
| die Grenze (-n) | border |
| die Bundesrepublik (Deutschland) (die BRD) | Federal Republic (of Germany) |
| die Deutsche Demokratische Republik (die DDR) | German Democratic Republic (1949–1990) (E Germany) |

| | |
|---|---|
| die Vereinigten Staaten von Amerika (*pl*) | United States of America |
| das Vereinigte Königreich | United Kingdom |
| die Europäische Union (die EU) | European Union |
| nach Deutschland/in Deutschland | to Germany/in Germany |
| in die Schweiz/in der Schweiz | to/in Switzerland |

| | |
|---|---|
| das Bundesland (¨er) | 'land': Federal State of Germany |
| Bayern | Bavaria |
| Köln | Cologne |
| Hannover | Hanover |
| München | Munich |
| Wien | Vienna |
| Genf | Geneva |

| | |
|---|---|
| das Meer (-e) }<br>die See } | sea |
| der Ozean (-e) | ocean |
| die Nordsee | North Sea |
| die Ostsee | Baltic Sea |
| das Mittelmeer | Mediterranean Sea |
| der Atlantik | Atlantic |
| der Pazifik | Pacific |
| der Kanal (¨e) | canal, channel |
| der Ärmelkanal | English Channel |
| die Insel (-n) | island |
| der See (-n) | lake |
| der Bodensee | Lake Constance |
| der Genfer See | Lake Geneva |
| der Fluß (Flüsse) | river |
| der Strom (¨e) | major river |
| der Rhein | Rhine |
| die Mosel | Mosel |
| die Donau | Danube |
| die Elbe | Elbe |
| die Themse | Thames |
| das Tal (¨er) | valley |
| das Rheintal | Rhine valley |
| der Berg (-e) | mountain, hill |
| der Hügel (-) | small hill |
| die Zugspitze | (*Germany's highest mountain*) |
| die Alpen | Alps |

## b Länder    Countries

*The masculine names for the inhabitants of these countries/areas are normal (strong) masculine nouns: the genitive ends in -s, and the plural is unchanged. The feminine name is formed by adding -in to the end of the masculine noun.*

| Land | country | Einwohner | Nationalität |
|---|---|---|---|
| Afrika | Africa | der Afrikaner | afrikanisch |
| Amerika | America | der Amerikaner | amerikanisch |
| Australien | Australia | der Australier | australisch |
| Belgien | Belgium | der Belgier | belgisch |
| England | England | der Engländer | englisch |
| Europa | Europe | der Europäer | europäisch |
| Holland | Holland | der Holländer | holländisch |
| Indien | India | der Inder | indisch |
| Italien | Italy | der Italiener | italienisch |
| Japan | Japan | der Japaner | japanisch |
| Kanada | Canada | der Kanadier | kanadisch |
| Luxemburg | Luxembourg | der Luxemburger | luxemburgisch |
| die Niederlande (*pl*) | Netherlands | der Niederländer | niederländisch |
| Neuseeland | New Zealand | der Neuseeländer | neuseeländisch |
| Norwegen | Norway | der Norweger | norwegisch |
| Österreich | Austria | der Österreicher | österreichisch |
| die Schweiz | Switzerland | der Schweizer | schweizerisch |
| Skandinavien | Scandinavia | der Skandinavier | skandinavisch |
| Spanien | Spain | der Spanier | spanisch |
| Wales | Wales | der Waliser | walisisch |

The masculine names for the inhabitants of these countries/areas decline weak: all parts except for the nominative singular for the masculine end in -n. The feminine name is formed by replacing the final -e of the masculine noun with -in.

| Land | country | Einwohner | Nationalität |
|------|---------|-----------|--------------|
| China | China | der Chinese | chinesisch |
| Dänemark | Denmark | der Däne | dänisch |
| Frankreich | France | der Franzose | französisch |
| Griechenland | Greece | der Grieche | griechisch |
| Großbritannien | Great Britain | der Brite | britisch |
| Irland | Ireland | der Ire | irisch |
| Polen | Poland | der Pole | polnisch |
| Portugal | Portugal | der Portugiese | portugiesisch |
| Rumänien | Romania | der Rumäne | rumänisch |
| Rußland | Russia | der Russe | russisch |
| Schottland | Scotland | der Schotte | schottisch |
| Schweden | Sweden | der Schwede | schwedisch |
| die Slowakei | Slovakia | der Slowake | slowakisch |
| die Türkei | Turkey | der Türke | türkisch |

One nationality noun declines like an adjective:

| Deutschland | Germany | der Deutsche/ die Deutsche | deutsch |
|-------------|---------|------------------------------|---------|

 See also May I introduce myself, pages 53–4.

## Jetzt bist du dran! 51

Schreib den Namen des dazugehörigen Landes auf die Linie neben seine Hauptstadt!

Write the name of each country on the line next to its capital city.

Bern:.....................

Lissabon:.....................

den Haag:.....................

Budapest:.....................  Rom:.....................

Stockholm:.....................  Prag:.....................

Kopenhagen:.....................  Warschau:.....................

Bucharest:.....................  Edinburg:.....................

Athen:.....................  Wien:.....................

Dublin:.....................  Paris:.....................

Brüssel:.....................  Oslo:.....................

London:.....................

Madrid:.....................

Berlin:.....................

### c Der Austausch — Exchange

| | |
|---|---|
| der Austausch | exchange |
| die Partnerstadt (¨e) | twin town |
| einladen (er lädt ... ein) (*s; sep*) | to invite |
| die Einladung (-en) | invitation |
| annehmen (er nimmt ... an) (*s; sep*) | to accept |
| ablehnen (*sep*) | to decline |
| bedauern (*insep*) | to regret |
| abholen (*sep*) | to fetch, meet (*at station etc*) |
| willkommen! | welcome! |
| möchten Sie etwas trinken/ essen? | would you like something to eat/drink? |
| Neues erleben (*insep*) | to see something new |

| | |
|---|---|
| **kennenlernen (*sep*)** | to get to know |
| **sich gewöhnen an (+*Acc*) (*insep*)** | to get used to |
| **der/die Fremde (*adj. noun*)** | stranger (*m/f*) |
| **der Ausländer/die Ausländerin** | foreigner (*m/f*) |
| **besichtigen (*insep*)** | to visit, look around |
| **einen Ausflug machen** | to go on a trip |

 See also Meeting people, pages 64–5 & Holidays, pages 100–7.

## d Die königliche Familie — The Royal Family

| | |
|---|---|
| **das Königreich (-e)** | kingdom |
| **der König (-e)** | king |
| **die Königin (-nen)** | queen |
| **der Prinz (-en)** | prince |
| **die Prinzessin (-nen)** | princess |
| **die Königinmutter** | queen mother |
| **der Herzog** | duke |
| **die Herzogin** | duchess |

## e Die Politik — Politics

| | |
|---|---|
| **der Staat (-en)** | state |
| **die Republik (-en)** | republic |
| **der Präsident (-en, -en)** | president (*m*) |
| **die Präsidentin (-nen)** | president (*f*) |
| **der Kanzler/Bundeskanzler (-)** | (federal) chancellor |
| **der Premierminister (-)** | prime minister (*m*) |
| **die Premierministerin (-nen)** | prime minister (*f*) |
| **der Minister (-)** | minister (*m*) |
| **die Ministerin (-nen)** | minister (*f*) |
| **der Diktator (-en)** / **die Diktatorin (-nen)** | dictator (*m/f*) |
| **regieren** | to rule |
| **die Regierung (-en)** | government |
| **das Parlament** | parliament |
| **der Bundesrat** / **der Bundestag** | two houses of German parliament |
| **der/die Abgeordnete (*adj. noun*)** | Member of Parliament (*m/f*) |
| **der Politiker (-)** | politician (*m*) |
| **die Politikerin (-nen)** | politician (*f*) |
| **vertreten (er vertritt) (*s; insep*)** | to represent |
| **die Verfassung (-en)** | constitution |
| **die Debatte (-n)** | debate |

| | |
|---|---|
| das Gesetz (-e) | law |
| ein Gesetz verabschieden (*insep*) | to pass a law |
| die Partei (-en) | party |
| die Opposition | opposition |
| die Demokratie | democracy |
| frei | free |
| die Freiheit (-en) | freedom |
| wählen | to elect, to vote |
| die Wahl (-en) | election, choice |
| der Wähler (-) | voter |
| der Wahlkreis (-e) | constituency |
| stimmen (für…) | to vote (for…) |
| die Stimme (-n) | vote |
| eine Mehrheit von 6 Stimmen haben | to have a majority of 6 votes |
| die Meinung (-en) | opinion |
| der Bürger (-) | citizen |

## Jetzt bist du dran! 52

*Mann kann hier Wörter über die Politik finden. Man liest nach oben oder nach unten, vorwärts oder rückwärts. Wenn du über 20 findest, ist das sehr gut.*

Find words about politics. They read up, down, forwards or backwards. If you can find over 20, you are doing very well.

| N | S | K | Ö | N | I | G | R | E | I | C | H |
|---|---|---|---|---|---|---|---|---|---|---|---|
| E | R | R | F | O | M | E | U | D | C | F | C |
| F | E | E | W | I | A | W | S | P | D | R | I |
| F | S | I | Ä | T | R | A | T | K | E | I | E |
| A | I | S | H | I | I | L | R | I | M | E | R |
| W | A | H | L | S | N | T | U | L | O | D | Z |
| M | K | E | E | O | E | L | P | B | K | E | T |
| O | M | E | R | P | N | A | P | U | R | N | E |
| T | D | R | A | P | O | N | E | P | A | L | S |
| A | B | G | E | O | R | D | N | E | T | E | E |
| T | A | D | I | D | N | A | K | R | I | E | G |
| G | A | T | S | E | D | N | U | B | E | R | B |

## f Die Ordnung — Law and order

| | |
|---|---|
| die Ordnung | law and order |
| die Bürgerinitiative (-n) | local interest-group |
| die Politik (*no pl*) | politics/policy |
| bedenken (er bedenkt) (*irreg w; insep*) | to consider |
| der Friede (-ns, -n) | peace |
| friedlich | peaceful(ly) |
| | |
| die Marine/Kriegsmarine | navy |
| der Matrose (-n, -n) | sailor |
| das Heer (-e) | army |
| die Armee (-n) | army |
| der Soldat (-en, -en) | soldier |
| die Luftwaffe | air force |
| | |
| der Krieg (-e) | war |
| den Notstand ausrufen (er ruft ... aus) (*s; sep*) | to declare a state of emergency |
| der Notfall (⁻e) | emergency |
| die Not (⁻e) | need, want |
| | |
| die Gewalt | power/violence |
| der Rassismus | racism |
| der Extremist (-en, -en) | extremist |
| der Terrorist (-en, -en) | terrorist |
| | |
| die Entführung (-en) | kidnapping |
| entführen (*insep*) | to hijack |
| die Geisel (-n) | hostage |
| jemanden als Geisel halten (er hält) (*s*) | to hold somebody to ransom |
| das Opfer (-) | victim |
| | |
| die Feuerpause (-n) | cease-fire |
| der Vertrag (⁻e) | treaty, agreement |
| Gespräche (n pl) | talks |
| der Bombenalarm (-e) | bomb scare |
| die Explosion (-en) | explosion |
| | |
| die Bombe (-n) | bomb |
| die Atomwaffe (-n) | atomic weapon |
| die Kernwaffe (-n) | nuclear weapon |

| | |
|---|---|
| demonstrieren (gegen +*Acc*) | to demonstrate (against...) |
| die Demonstration (-en) | demonstration |
| protestieren (gegen + *Acc*) | to protest (against...) |

### g Die Dritte Welt — Third World

| | |
|---|---|
| der Hunger | hunger |
| der Durst | thirst |
| die Hungersnot | famine |
| die Dürre (-n) | drought |
| die Armut | poverty |

### h Die Diplomatie — Diplomacy

| | |
|---|---|
| die Welt (-en) | world |
| die Europäische Union | European Union |
| (die) NATO | NATO |
| (die) UNO | UN |
| der Außenminister (-) | Foreign Secretary |
| der/die Delegierte (*adj. noun*) | delegate (*m/f*) |
| verhandeln (*insep*) | to negotiate |
| die Verhandlungen (*pl*) | negotiations |
| die Warnung (-en) | warning |
| vermeiden (er vermeidet) (*s*) | to avoid |
| der Stellvertreter (-)<br>die Stellvertreterin (-nen) } | representative (*m/f*) |
| der Sprecher (-)<br>die Sprecherin (-nen) } | spokesman/-woman |
| der Botschafter (-)<br>die Botschafterin (-nen) } | ambassador (*m/f*) |
| die Botschaft (-en) | embassy |
| das Konsulat (-e) | consulate |
| der Konsul (-n) | consul (*m*) |
| die Konsulin (-nen) | consul (*f*) |

## Einige nützliche Wörter

## Some essential little words

| | |
|---|---|
| (irgend)ein, -e, - | any |
| ab und zu | now and again |
| aber | but |
| allerlei | all sorts of |
| alles klar | OK |
| als ob | as though |
| also, ... | well, ... |
| also | therefore |
| am meisten | most of all |
| andere (r, s) | other |
| äußerst | extremely |
| auch | also |
| bald | soon |
| beinahe | almost |
| besonders | especially |
| besser | better |
| bestimmt | certain |
| ein bißchen | a little |
| bitte | please, here you are, you're welcome |
| damit | so that |
| danach | then, after that |
| danke | thank you |
| dann | then |
| das heißt (dh) | that is to say (ie) |
| denn | for, because |
| deshalb | so, therefore |
| doch! | yes! (*contradicting a negative*) |
| dort | there |
| einmal | once |
| einschließlich | including |
| endlich | finally, eventually |
| entlang (+Acc after noun) | along |
| entweder ... oder | either ... or |
| erst | only (*referring to time*) |

| | |
|---|---|
| es geht um | it's a question of |
| es gibt | there is/are |
| etwa | approximately |
| etwas | something |
| etwas anderes | something else |
| falls | if, in case |
| fast | almost |
| fort | away, gone |
| früh | early |
| ganz | entirely |
| gar nicht | not at all |
| gar nichts | nothing at all |
| genug | enough |
| gut | good |
| hier | here |
| hoch | high, high up |
| immer | always |
| inzwischen | meanwhile |
| irgendwo | anywhere |
| ja | yes |
| jawohl | yes, indeed |
| jeder, jede, jedes | each |
| jedenfalls | anyhow |
| jedermann | everyone |
| jedoch | however |
| jemand | someone |
| jetzt | now |
| kein, keine, kein | not any |
| lange | for a long time |
| leider | unfortunately |
| manchmal | sometimes |
| mehr | more |
| mehrere | several |
| meistens | mostly |
| mindestens } wenigstens } | at least |
| mitten in | in the middle of (something) |
| nachher | afterwards |
| natürlich | of course |
| nein | no |

| | | | |
|---|---|---|---|
| nicht | not | wann? | when? |
| nichts | nothing | warum? | why? |
| nicht mehr | no longer | was? | what? |
| nie | never | weder ... noch | neither ... nor |
| niemand | nobody | wegen | because of |
| nirgendwo | nowhere | weil | because |
| nochmals | again | weit | a long way, far |
| noch nicht | not yet | weit entfernt | |
| normalerweise | normally | (von) | far (from) |
| nur | only | welcher, welche, | |
| obwohl | although | welches | which |
| oder | or | weniger | less |
| oft | often | wenn | if, whenever |
| plötzlich | suddenly | wer? | who? |
| schlecht | bad | wie, bitte? | pardon? |
| sehr | very | wieviel? | how much? |
| selten | not often, seldom | wie viele? | how many? |
| | | wieder | again |
| sicher! | of course! | wieso? | why, how come? |
| sogar | even | wirklich | really |
| sondern | but (*after a negative*) | wo? | where? |
| | | woher? | where ... from? |
| spät | late | wohin? | where (to)? |
| statt | instead of | zB | eg |
| trotz | in spite of | zu (viel) | too (much) |
| überall | everywhere | zuerst | first of all |
| und | and | zum Glück | fortunately |
| usw | etc | zunächst | firstly |
| viel | much, a lot | zusammen | together |
| vor kurzem | recently | zwar | admittedly |
| während | while | | |

# Einige nützliche Verben

# Some useful verbs

| | |
|---|---|
| aufhören (*sep*) | to stop |
| aufmachen (*sep*) | to open |
| ausgehen* (*s; sep*) | to go out |
| beenden (*insep*) | to finish |
| benutzen (*insep*) | to use |
| danken (*+Dat*) | to thank |
| denken (*irr w*) | to think |
| dürfen (*irreg*) | to be allowed to |
| (sich) entscheiden (*s*) (*insep*) | to decide |
| essen (*s*) | to eat |
| geben (*s*) | to give |
| gefallen (*s*) (*+Dat*) | to please, appeal to |
| gehen* (*s*) | to go |
| (zu Fuß) gehen* (*s*) | to walk |
| gern haben }<br>mögen (*irreg*) } | to like |
| glauben | to believe |
| gucken/schauen | to look |
| haben (*irreg w*) | to have |
| helfen (*s*) (*+Dat*) | to help |
| hinstellen/hinsetzen (*sep*) | to put (*down*) |
| hören | to hear |
| kaufen | to buy |
| kennen (*irr w*) | to know (*person, place*) |
| kommen*(*s*) | to come |
| können (*irreg*) | to be able |
| laufen* (*s*) | to run, go on foot |
| machen | to do, make |
| meinen | to think, mean, say |
| müssen (*irreg*) | must, to have to |
| nehmen (*s*) | to take |
| passieren* | to happen |
| sagen | to say |
| schließen (*s*) }<br>zumachen (*sep*) } | to close |
| sehen (*s*) | to see |
| sein* (*irreg s*) | to be |
| sich setzen | to sit down |
| sitzen (*s*) | to be sitting down |
| sollen (*irreg*) | should, be supposed to |
| stecken | to put (*push inside*) |
| sterben* (*s*) | to die |

| | |
|---|---|
| vergessen (*s*) | to forget |
| verkaufen (*insep*) | to sell |
| verlassen (*s; insep*) | to leave |
| verlieren (*s; insep*) | to lose |
| versprechen (*s; insep*) | to promise |
| verstehen (*s; insep*) | to understand |
| wählen | to choose |
| weitermachen (*w; sep*) | to continue/carry on |
| werden\*(*irreg*) | to become |
| wissen (*irreg*) | to know (*facts*) |
| wollen (*irreg*) | to want, wish |
| zeigen | to show |
| zurückgehen\*/zurückkommen\* (*s; sep*) | to return, go back to |
| zurückfahren\* (*s*) | to return, drive back |

## Einige nützliche Adjektive

## Some useful adjectives

| | | | |
|---|---|---|---|
| besser | better | möglich | possible |
| breit | wide | naß | wet |
| durchschnittlich | average | nötig | necessary |
| einfach | easy | nützlich | useful |
| eng | narrow, tight | nutzlos | useless, pointless |
| ernst | serious | praktisch | practical |
| fertig | ready, finished | schlecht | bad |
| feucht | damp | schwer | heavy, difficult |
| gut | good | selten | rare |
| leer | empty | sympathisch | kind |
| leicht | light, easy | voll | full |

## Die Farben

## Colours

| | | | |
|---|---|---|---|
| blau | blue | schwarz | black |
| blond | blond | silber | silver |
| braun | brown | türkis | turquoise |
| gelb | yellow | violett | violet |
| golden | gold, golden | weiß | white |
| grau | grey | bunt | colourful |
| grün | green | dunkel | dark |
| lila | lilac | hell | light |
| orange | orange | dunkelblau/ | dark blue/ |
| rosa | pink | hellblau usw | light blue etc |
| rot | red | | |

# Examination Rubrics

|  |  |
|---|---|
| Äußern Sie sich dazu | Respond |
| Beantworten Sie die Fragen auf deutsch | Answer the questions in German |
| Für jede Frage haben Sie vier Antworten zur Auswahl | For each question you have a choice of four answers |
| Sie brauchen nicht alle Buchstaben | You don't need all the letters |
| Benutzen Sie diese Symbole | Use these symbols |
| Bitte wenden<br>Blättern Sie bitte um | Please turn over |
| Bringen Sie die Sätze (die Wörter) in die richtige (eine sinnvolle) Reihenfolge | Put the sentences (words) into the correct order |
| Wie ist die richtige Reihenfolge? | What is the correct order? |
| Ergänzen Sie den Zeitplan | Complete the timetable |
| Finden Sie die Wörter | Find the words |
| Füllen Sie die Lücken<br>die Tabelle<br>das Formular aus<br>den Fragebogen | Fill in the gaps<br>grid<br>form<br>survey |
| Geben Sie Auskünfte über... | Give information about... |
| Haken Sie (den richtigen Buchstaben) ab | Tick (the correct letter) |
| in Ziffern | in numbers |
| als Liste | as a list |
| Korrigieren Sie die Notiz<br>Schreiben Sie die Notiz richtig | Correct the notice |
| Kreuzen Sie das entsprechende Kästchen (die Lösung) an | Tick the corresponding box (answer) |
| Lesen Sie den (folgenden) Artikel durch | Read through the (following) article |
| Kreisen Sie Ja oder Nein | Circle yes or no |
| Machen Sie Notizen | Make notes |
| Markieren Sie, ob A, B, C oder D richtig ist | Indicate whether A, B, C or D is correct |
| Notieren Sie die Einzelheiten | Take down the details |
| Ordnen Sie die Sätze richtig ein/zu | Put the sentences into order |
| Richtig oder falsch? | True or false? |
| Schreiben Sie die richtigen Nummern neben die Bilder | Write the correct numbers next to the pictures |

| | |
|---|---|
| **Schreiben Sie einen Bericht über...** | Write a report on... |
| **einen Brief an...** | a letter to... |
| **Ihre Meinung zu/über...** | your opinion on... |
| **Schreiben Sie einen Dialog zum Thema...** | Make up a dialogue on the theme of... |
| | |
| **Sehen Sie (die Zeichnungen) an** | Look at (the drawings) |
| **Sie besprechen...** | They are discussing... |
| **Sie dürfen ein Wörterbuch verwenden** | You may use a dictionary |
| **Stellen Sie sich vor** | Introduce yourself |
| **Tragen sie den Namen in die Tabelle ein** | Write the name in the grid |
| **Übersetzen Sie ins Englische** | Translate into English |
| **Verbinden Sie...** | Match up... |
| **Was paßt zusammen?** | What goes together? |
| **Wählen Sie die passende Beschreibung/die Beschreibung, die am besten paßt** | Choose the description that best fits |
| **Welche Schlagzeile paßt zu welchem Thema?** | Which headline goes with which topic? |
| **Wählen Sie die richtige Antwort** | Choose the right answer |
| **Was bedeuten diese Symbole?** | What do these symbols mean? |
| **Was fehlt hier?** | What is missing here? |
| **Was trifft zu?** | What is correct? |
| **Was wird angeboten?** | What is on offer? |
| **Zeichnen Sie einen Pfeil** | Draw an arrow |
| | |
| **Ändern Sie...** | Change... |
| **Begrüßen Sie...** | Greet... |
| **Beschreiben Sie...** | Describe... |
| **Erfinden Sie...** | Invent... |
| **Erklären Sie...** | Explain... |
| **Erzählen Sie, (was passiert ist)** | Give an account (of what happened) |
| | |
| **Gehen Sie ... nochmal durch** | Check... |
| **Schauen Sie ... an** | Look at... |
| **Schlagen Sie ... vor** | Suggest... |
| **Stellen Sie sich vor, ...** | Imagine... |
| **Unterstreichen Sie...** | Underline... |
| **Vergleichen Sie...** | Compare... |
| **Wiederholen Sie** | Repeat |

| | |
|---|---|
| **Bevor Sie das Gespräch hören** | Before listening to the conversation |
| **Hören Sie (gut) zu** | Listen (carefully) |
| **Hören Sie sich das Interview/ Beispiel an** | Listen to the interview/example |
| **Jezt hören Sie eine Sendung** | Now you will hear a programme |
| **einige Bemerkungen** | some comments |
| **Zwei Personen reden/sprechen über...** | Two people are talking about... |
| **Während Sie zuhören...** | While you are listening... |
| **Begrüßen Sie...** | Greet... |
| **Nehmen Sie Abschied vom Lehrer** | Say goodbye to your teacher |
| **Erkündigen Sie sich über folgendes** | Ask for the following information |
| **Fragen Sie nach...** | Make inquiries about... |
| **Stellen Sie Fragen über...** | Ask questions about... |
| **Melden Sie sich** | Say who you are (*on the phone*) |
| **Sagen Sie ihm/ihr/ihnen** | Tell him/her/them |

 ## Jetzt bist du dran! 53

| Find die Buchstaben, die das Ende des ersten Wortes und auch der Anfang des zweiten Wortes sind! | Find the letters which end the first word and begin the second. |
|---|---|

| **Beispiel:** | SIE*** | Nummer | = *sieben* |
| | ***ZIN | fürs Auto | = *Benzin* |

*Leicht/Easy:*

| 1 | TRIN*** | Wir ___ Wasser |
| | ***NEN | Wir ___ deine Eltern nicht |
| 2 | GUL*** | ungarischer Eintopf |
| | ***CHENBECHER | für Zigaretten |
| 3 | FÜH*** | vor den anderen gehen |
| | ***NEN | laufen |
| 4 | K***** | Geld dafür geben |
| | *****THALT | Urlaub |
| 5 | APPA*** | Kamera |
| | ***HAUS | wichtiges Gebäude im Stadtzentrum |
| 6 | KÜ*** | Strand |
| | ***RN | am Himmel |
| 7 | TI*** | Möbel |
| | ***UH | Man trägt ihn am Fuß |

➡

| | | |
|---|---|---|
| 8 | B*** | Wo man Geld bekommt |
| | ***OMMEN | da sein |
| 9 | VERKEHRS****** | Warnung auf der Straße |
| | ******KRÖTE | Haustier |
| 10 | FERNSE*** | Man findet es im Wohnzimmer |
| | ***Z | Körperteil |

Schwerer/Harder:

| | | |
|---|---|---|
| 11 | KR*** | Er ist rund |
| | ***EN | Metall |
| 12 | B*** | Farbe |
| | ***T | viel Lärm |
| 13 | H*** | Gebäude |
| | ***GANG | die Tür |
| 14 | L**** | Licht |
| | ****L | drei Lichter |
| 15 | B*** | farbig |
| | ***EN | im Erdgeschoß |
| 16 | B*** | Körperteil |
| | ***STIEG | die Tür, durch die man in den Bus steigt |
| 17 | B***** | über dem Fluß |
| | *****N | Körperteil |
| 18 | D*** | oben auf dem Haus |
| | ***TUNG | Vorsicht! |
| 19 | GE***** | Teil eines Essens |
| | *****IG | Stimmt! |
| 20 | Z**** | Körperteil |
| | ****RN | Es gefällt mir nicht; ich tue es _____ |

Die Schwersten/The hardest:

| | | |
|---|---|---|
| 21 | EIN***** | Komm zu uns! |
| | ***** | Geschäft |
| 22 | SCH***** | Wo man Fahrkarten kauft |
| | ***** | Wie alt man ist. |
| 23 | S***** | Rad vor dem Fahrer im Wagon |
| | ***** | Kostet viel |
| 24 | R**** | Bücherbrett |
| | **** | ganz unwichtig |
| 25 | Z***** | Raum |
| | ***** | die ganze Zeit |
| 26 | R**** | Geld für Alte |
| | **** | Vogel |
| 27 | M***** | Wir ____ die Temperatur |
| | ***** | Alle Menschen und Tiere machen es, um zu leben |
| 28 | K***** | ____ Sie die Briefmarke auf den Umschlag! |
| | ***** | existieren |

# Answers

**Jetzt bist du dran! 1**
1 Heute ist Mittwoch; 2 Heute ist
Montag; 3 Heute ist Samstag/
Sonnabend; 4 Heute ist Freitag;
5 Heute ist Dienstag; 6 Heute ist
Donnerstag; 7 Heute ist Sonntag.

**Jetzt bist du dran! 2**
1 Es ist Mittag; es ist Mitternacht;
2 Es ist neun Uhr fünfundvierzig or es
ist Viertel vor zehn; es ist
einundzwanig Uhr fünfundvierzig;
3 Es ist acht Uhr zwanzig or es ist
zwanzig nach acht; es ist zwanzig
Uhr zwanzig; 4 Es ist zehn Uhr
dreißig or es ist halb elf; es ist
zweiundzwanzig Uhr dreißig; 5 Es ist
sechs Uhr fünfzehn or es ist Viertel
nach sechs; es ist achtzehn Uhr
fünfzehn; 6 Es ist sieben Uhr; es ist
neunzehn Uhr; 7 Es ist vier Uhr
fünfunddreißig or es ist
fünfundzwanzig vor fünf; es ist
sechzehn Uhr fünfunddreißig; 8 Es ist
elf Uhr fünfzig or es ist zehn vor
zwölf; es ist dreiundzwanzig Uhr
fünfzig; 9 Es ist drei Uhr
fünfundzwnzig or es ist
fünfundzwanzig nach drei; es ist
fünfzehn Uhr fünfundzwanzig;
10 Es ist vierundzwanzig Uhr fünf; es
ist zwölf Uhr fünf or es ist fünf nach
zwölf.

**Jetzt bist du dran! 3**
1 dreißig; 2 achtundachtzig;
3 fünfundsechzig; 4 zweihundert;
5 eintausendachthundertundsechzig;
6 hunderteins; 7 einundsiebzig;
8 achtzig; 9 einundneunzig;
10 zweihunderttausend.

**Jetzt bist du dran! 4**
1 ich dusche ; 2 ich putze mir die
Zähne; 3 ich ziehe mich an; 4 ich
kämme mich; 5 ich gehe nach unten;
6 ich frühstücke; 7 ich mache mich
fertig or ich packe die Schulsachen;
8 ich verlasse das Haus.

**Jetzt bist du dran! 5**
Use whatever phrases apply to your
own circumstances.

**Jetzt bist du dran! 6**
Use whatever phrases apply to your
own circumstances.

**Jetzt bist du dran! 7**
1=c; 2=e; 3=g; 4=f; 5=a; 6=b; 7=d.

**Jetzt bist du dran! 8**
das Pult – das Klassenzimmer; die
Bank – das Labor; die Federballnetze
– die Turnhalle; die Mäntel – die
Garderobe; das Geschirr – der
Speisesaal; die Umkleidekabinen –
das Schwimmbad.

**Jetzt bist du dran! 9**
Use whatever phrases apply to your
own circumstances.

**Jetzt bist du dran! 10**
Use whatever phrases apply to your
own circumstances.

**Jetzt bist du dran! 11**
Your answers will depend on your
own cirmcumstances.

**Jetzt bist du dran! 12**
Use whatever phrases apply to your
own circumstances.

**Jetzt bist du dran! 13**
Eins; Speisesaal; Klassenbuch;
Lieblingsfach; Informatik; Nebenfach;
Garderobe; Erdkunde; Labor;
Taschenrechner (ES KLINGELT).

**Jetzt bist du dran! 14**
1 die Banane; 2 der Kuchen;
3 der Fisch; 4 das Hähnchen;
5 die Ananas; 6 das Brot; 7 der Käse;
8 das Spiegelei; 9 die Birne;
10 die Pommes frites; 11 die Möhre
or die Karotte; 12 zwei Kirschen.

**Jetzt bist du dran! 15**
Aufschnitt; Bonbon; Curry; Dose;
Erbse; Forelle; Gans; hartgekocht;
Imbiß; Joghurt; Knoblauch; Limone;
Möhre; Nuß; Omelett; Pilze; Quark;
Rührei; Senf; Tomate; ungesund;
Vollmilch; Wurst; Zwiebel.

### Jetzt bist du dran! 16
1 alt/dick; 2 scharf; 3 kalt; schmeckt; 4 Riegel; darf/sollte; 5 Löffeln Zucker; süß; 6 Ahnung; probiert; 7 will/kann; alt; sauer; 8 schmeckt dieser; scharf/unappetitlich.

### Jetzt bist du dran! 17
Girl: die Stirn; die Nase; der Mund; das Kinn; die Schulter; die Hand; die Taille; die Hüfte; das Bein; der Fuß; Boy: das Haar; das Ohr; die Wange; der Hals; der Arm; die Brust; der Ellenbogen; der Magen/der Bauch; das Handgelenk; das Knie; der Knöchel.

### Jetzt bist du dran! 18
1 Die Hand/Der Arm/Die Schulter (etc) tut mir weh; 2 Die Füße tun mir weh; 3 Die Augen tun mir weh; 4 Der Fuß tut mir weh/Die Zehen tun mir weh; 5 Der Rücken tut mir weh; 6 Das Bein tut mir weh; 7 Die Nase tut mir weh; 8 Der Kopf tut mir weh; 9 Die Zähne tun mir weh. 10 Der Hals tut mir weh.

### Jetzt bist du dran! 19
Fill in the form with your personal details.

### Jetzt bist du dran! 20
1 Neffe; 2 Großmutter; 3 Enkelin; 4 Vetter/Cousin; 5 Großeltern; 6 Stiefvater; 7 Schwägerin; 8 Schwiegereltern; 9 Zwillingsbruder; 10 Halbschwester.

### Jetzt bist du dran! 21
Use whatever phrases apply to your own circumstances.

### Jetzt bist du dran! 22
Use whatever phrases apply to your own cirmcumstances.

### Jetzt bist du dran! 23
Bart; Beine; blond; dünn; egoistisch; frech; Genie; Haare; hell; höflich; hübsch; interessant; Kopf; Körper; lachen, Laune; Lid; lockig; lustig, nett; Neugier; schön; stark; sympathisch; toll; traurig; unhöflich; wellig; Zahn; Zehe; Zunge.

### Jetzt bist du dran! 24
1 groß, altmodisch, ein Einfamilienhaus; 2 vier Stockwerke, einen Dachboden, Schornsteine; 3 einen kleinen Garten.

### Jetzt bist du dran! 25
1 Es steht einen Kochtopf mit einen Löffel auf dem Herd; 2 Es liegt ein Buch auf dem Couchtisch. Ein Sessel steht neben dem Fenster; 3 Es gibt ein Bett und einen Nachttisch mit einer Lampe, einem Wecker und einem Paar Pantoffeln; 4 Da ist ein Waschbecken, ein Brett mit einer Zahnbürste darauf, und ein Spiegel; 5 Es gibt einen Stuhl, einen Arbeitstisch, einen Computer, Bücher, ein Bücherregal, und ein Telefon; 6 Dort steht eine Tasse, eine Untertasse und ein Glas auf dem Tisch.

### Jetzt bist du dran! 26
1 Computer; 2 Apparat; 3 Spiegel; 4 Untertasse; 5 Schublade; 6 Anrichte; 7 Badewanne; 8 Lautsprecher; 9 Gasherd; 10 Staubsauger.

### Jetzt bist du dran! 27
Use whatever phrases apply to your own circumstances.

### Jetzt bist du dran! 28
**Across:** Käfig; Pferd; Meerschweinchen; Schildkröte.
**Down:** Maus; Katze; Goldfisch; Kaninchen.

### Jetzt bist du dran! 29
Hast du Lust, mit mir ins Konzert zu gehen? Was hast du eigentlich Freitag abend vor? Willst du nachher ins China-Restaurant? Ich lade dich zu einer Fete bei Heinz ein. Udo ist langweilig; er macht nie mit! Ich habe die Karten für die Aufführung schon gekauft. Ich schlage etwas Interessantes vor. Wir wollen

zusammen das Ende des Semesters feiern. Ich habe aber leider schon all mein Taschengeld ausgegeben. Die Disco in der Talstraße hat heute abend ja zu! Marianne hat mir den Film sehr empfohlen. Ich muß mir aber unbedingt die Haare waschen!

### Jetzt bist du dran! 30
**1** Fußball; Tennis; **2** Schwimmen; **3** Ski; **4** Rugby; **5** Disco/Disko /Discothek.

### Jetzt bist du dran! 31
**1** Neujahr; **2** der Heilige Abend; **3** der erste Weihnachtstag; **4** der zweite Weihnachtstag; **5** Silvester.

### Jetzt bist du dran! 32
Wir packten die Koffer alle ins Auto. Das Luftkissenfahrzeug fährt schon um 10.30 Uhr ab. Wir dürfen den Fotoapparat nicht vergessen! Wir haben die Schiffskarten schon im voraus gekauft. Wir wollen durch den Tunnel nach Brüssel fahren. Man muß eine gute Stunde vor der Abfahrtszeit da sein. Du brauchst ja keine Angst vor der Landung zu haben. Wir haben vor, unterwegs in Straßburg zu übernachten. Wir suchen kein sehr teures Hotel. Der Herbergsvater bat um unsere Ausweise. Die Campingplätze sind im Juli oft voll belegt. Der Fahrstuhl im Hotel war leider außer Betrieb.

### Jetzt bist du dran! 33
die Bar – der Schnaps; die Kellnerin – die Bedienung; der Aufzug – außer Betrieb; das Zimmer – die Übernachtung; der Parkplatz – die Tiefgarage; der Balkon – die Aussicht; die Anmeldung – die Empfangsdame; der Gepäckträger – der Koffer; die Rechnung – die Abreise; das Formular – die Unterschrift; der Schlafraum – der Schlafsack; die Batterie – die Taschenlampe; die Dusche – der Waschraum; die Platzruhe – Mitternacht; klappbar – der Stuhl; das Zelt – aufschlagen; das Geschirr – die Spülküche; die Gebühr – zahlen;

wandern – der Rucksack; das Mitglied – der Ausweis.

### Jetzt bist du dran! 34
**1** das Gepäck; **2** der Ausweis; die Fahrkarte; **3** der Klappstuhl; der Campingkocher; der Kochtopf; **4** der Liegestuhl; **5** der Tourist.

### Jetzt bist du dran! 35
a = 8; b = 6; c = 2; d = 9; e = 1; f = 5; g = 4; h = 3; i = 7.

### Jetzt bist du dran! 36
die Brücke – der Fluß; die Ampel – die Kreuzung; eine Turnhalle – das Sportzentrum; der Bahnsteig – der Bahnhof; die Broschüre – das Verkehrsbüro; die Verkäuferin – das Warenhaus; der Turm – die Kirche; das Hochhaus – der neue Stadtteil; Obst – der Markt.

### Jetzt bist du dran! 37
**1** zum Bahnhof; **2** zur Post/zum Postamt; **3** zur Polizeiwache; **4** zum Kino; **5** zum Café; **6** zum Markt; **7** zur Kirche; **8** zum Schwimmbad/ Hallenbad/Freibad; **9** zum Stadion.

### Jetzt bist du dran! 38
Bach; Bau; Bauer; Bauernhaus; Bauernhof; Berg; Biene; Bock; Brücke; Dorf; Ebene; Ei; Eiche; Feld; Gebirge; Gipfel; Gras; Grün; Hecke; Heu; Hügel; Huhn; Insel; Kaninchen; Kuh; Lamm; Land; Landschaft; Nest; Reh; Schaf; Scheune; See; Stall; Tal; Tanne; Ufer; Vogel; Wald; Weg; Wiese; Zaun; Ziege.

### Jetzt bist du dran! 39
**1** forecast; **2** rise; **3** overcast; **4** sky; **5** thunderstorm; (FROST).

### Jetzt bist du dran! 40
**1** Schatten; **2** Aufheiterungen; **3** stark/stürmisch; **4** Blitz; **5** Nebel; **6** Wettervorhersage; werden; **7** gefroren; Glatteis; **8** Regen; trocken; **9** bewölkt; **10** Schauer; scheint.

**Jetzt bist du dran! 41**
1 der Juwelier; 2 die Konditorei;
3 die Fleischerei/die Metzgerei;
4 die Apotheke; 5 die
Schreibwarenhandlung/das
Schreibwarengeschäft; 6 die Bäckerei;
7 der Zeitungshändler/der
Zeitungsstand; 8 der Süßwarenladen;
9 das Warenhaus/das Kaufhaus/die
Drogerie.

**Jetzt bist du dran! 42**
1 Blumengeschäft; 2 Bäckerei;
3 Fischgeschäft;
4 Bekleidungsgeschäft;
5 Metzgerei/Fleischerei;
6 Schreibwarenhandlung; 7 Drogerie;
8 Apotheke; 9 Konditorei;
10 Süßwarenladen.

**Jetzt bist du dran! 43**
1 eng; 2 bar; 3 darf; 4 Stück;
5 Nummer; 6 empfehlen;
7 Abteilung; 8 Kasse; 9 geschlossen;
10 durchgehend; 11 bedienen;
12 umsonst; 13 umtauschen;
14 zeigen; 15 ausgeben

**Jetzt bist du dran! 44**
1 die Jeans; 2 der Mantel; 3 der Rock;
4 die Mütze; 5 das Kleid; 6 die
Strumpfhose; 7 die Halskette; 8 die
Socke; 9 der Gürtel; 10 der Anorak;
11 der Hut; 12 die Stiefel.

**Jetzt bist du dran! 45**
1 Ampel; 2 Straßenarbeiten;
3 Flugzeuge; Flughafens;
4 Stundenkilometer fahren;
5 Richtung; 6 überholen; 7 Kinder;
Schule; 8 Zug; 9 Zebrastreifen;
10 halten.

**Jetzt bist du dran! 46**
Give your personal opinion on the
advantages and disadvantages of
each of the forms of transport.

**Jetzt bist du dran! 47**
die Panne – die Verspätung; die
Gepäckannahme – der Koffer; die
Kontrolle – der Schaffner; das Gleis –
die Abfahrt; einchecken – das
Flugticket; Straßenarbeiten – die
Geschwindigkeitsbeschränkung; der
Sturm – die Seekrankheit; abfliegen –
landen; sich anschnallen – der
Sicherheitsgurt; die Tankstelle – die
Zapfsäule; der Fahrplan – die
Auskunft; einsteigen – sich hinsetzen.

**Jetzt bist du dran! 48**
1 Briefträger; 2 Kellnerin;
3 Schaffner; 4 Friseurin;
5 Schiedsrichter; 6 Stewardeß;
7 Polizist; 8 Lehrerin; 9 Koch;
10 Musikerin.

**Jetzt bist du dran 49**
1 reich; 2 Arbeitsamt; 3 Betrieb;
4 Gehalt/Lohn; 5 Kollege/Kollegin;
6 verdient; 7 Chefin;
8 Fabrikarbeiter; 9 einstellen;
10 berufstätig.

**Jetzt bist du dran! 50**
Bild; Bit; booten; Buchstaben; Chip;
Computer; Daten; Festplatte; fett;
Kapitälchen; kursiv; Maus; Netz;
Panne; PC; speichern; Spiel; Stil; Taste;
tippen; verarbeiten; Virus.

**Jetzt bist du dran! 51**
Bern – die Schweiz; Lissabon –
Portugal; Den Haag – die
Niederlande; Budapest – Ungarn;
Stockholm – Schweden; Kopenhagen
– Dänemark; Bucharest – Rumänien;
Athen – Griechenland; Dublin –
Irland; Brüssel – Belgien; London –
Großbritannien; Madrid – Spanien;
Berlin – Deutschland; Rom – Italien;
Prag – die Tschechische Republik;
Warschau – Polen; Edinburg –
Schottland; Wien – Österreich; Paris –
Frankreich; Oslo – Norwegen.

**Jetzt bist du dran! 52**
Abgeordnete; APO; Atomwaffen;
Bundestag; CDU; Demokratie; EG;
Frieden; Gesetz; Gewalt; Heer; Kaiser;
Kandidat; Königreich; Kreis; Krieg;
Land; Marine; MdB; Opposition;
Reich; Republik; SPD; Truppen; Urne;
Wahl; Wähler.

**Jetzt bist du dran! 53**
**1** KEN; **2** ASCH; **3** REN; **4** AUFEN;
**5** RAT; **6** STE; **7** SCH; **8** ANK;
**9** SCHILD; **10** HER; **11** EIS; **12** LAU;
**13** AUS; **14** AMPE; **15** UNT; **16** EIN;
**17** RÜCKE; **18** ACH; **19** RICHT;
**20** UNGE; **21** LADEN; **22** ALTER;
**23** TEUER; **24** EGAL; **25** IMMER;
**26** ENTE; **27** ESSEN; **28** LEBEN.